EFFORTLESS
EGGLESS
BAKING

EFFORTLESS EGGLESS

100 Easy
& Creative
Recipes

for
Baking
without Eggs

Baking

Mimi Council

Countryman Press

An Imprint of W. W. Norton & Company
Celebrating a Century of Independent Publishing

Background linen texture: natthanim /
    iStock Photo

For information about permission to
reproduce selections from this book,
write to Permissions, Countryman Press,
500 Fifth Avenue, New York, NY 10110

For information about special discounts
for bulk purchases, please contact
W. W. Norton Special Sales at
specialsales@wwnorton.com or
800-233-4830

Manufacturing by Versa Press
Book design by Mia Johnson
Production manager: Devon Zahn

Countryman Press
www.countrymanpress.com

An imprint of
W. W. Norton & Company, Inc.
500 Fifth Avenue, New York, NY 10110
www.wwnorton.com

Library of Congress Cataloging-in-
    Publication Data

Names: Council, Mimi, author.
Title: Effortless eggless baking : 100 easy &
    creative recipes for baking without eggs /
    Mimi Council.
Description: New York : Countryman Press,
    an imprint of W. W. Norton & Company
    Independent Publishers since 1923, [2023] |
    Includes index.
Identifiers: LCCN 2022019509 |
    ISBN 9781682686829 (cloth) |
    ISBN 9781682686836 (epub)
Subjects: LCSH: Egg-free diet—Recipes. |
    Food allergy—Diet therapy—Recipes. |
    Baking. | LCGFT: Cookbooks.
Classification: LCC RM232 .C68 2022 | DDC
    641.5/6318—dc23/eng/20220629
LC record available at https://lccn.loc
    .gov/2022019509

10 9 8 7 6 5 4 3 2 1

For Otto,

*as my allergy-friendly baking
truly started with you*

CONTENTS

Introduction

Eggless baking. Two words that may seem like they don't belong together. Two words that may seem intimidating. You may be thinking, *Don't you need eggs to bake a cake? Cookies? Brownies?*

If you've ever purchased boxed versions of any of these popular desserts from the grocery store, then you know one of the main additional ingredients you need is eggs. That may have led you to believe that eggs are a crucial ingredient in these baked goods. Otherwise, the boxed versions would be ready to go sans eggs, right? Well, I will let you in on a little secret: Eggs are not required or even crucial to bake some of your favorite desserts! Not only that, those desserts can be just as delicious (if not more so) than their egg-filled friends.

You may be wondering if I eat eggs. And you may already know the answer to that if you've read my other books. The answer is absolutely yes; I eat eggs. Thankfully, I've been pretty lucky in my life in that it wasn't until my late 20s that I had to face challenges with food allergies. That's when I discovered I'm allergic to tapioca, which fortunately isn't as common an ingredient as eggs in baked goods. Because of my own food allergy I can empathize with people who have them too. And even before I discovered my own food allergy, and way

before I opened my bake shop, I was baking gluten-free cookies for my friends with a gluten allergy.

I believe everyone should have the opportunity to enjoy desserts *no matter what.* And it's for this reason that I've always been as inclusive as possible in my baking. When creating recipes for my blog I've always catered to people whose diets are vegan, gluten-free, egg-free, nut-free, and more. I develop and taste test each and every one of those recipes as someone who eats all the ingredients I'm leaving out. I like to consider myself the best taste tester in this sense. In the case of the recipes in this book, I know what these treats taste like *with* eggs, so I have gotten as close to that version as possible *without* the eggs.

The end game is this: I want you to make one of these eggless recipes, say for Chocolate Chip Cookies (page 95), take a bite, and declare, *That's a good cookie,* not *That's a good eggless cookie.* And in fact, people have said that very thing to me. I have had customers who are perfectly capable of eating eggs ask for and order this eggless cookie—it's that good. I created this recipe during the COVID-19 quarantine, when many people were out of eggs. I was getting texts and emails from people with lists of random ingredients asking me for a baking recipe using those random ingredients. This served as a source of inspiration, and so, while eggs were in short supply, I created an eggless cookie recipe. In all honestly, I wasn't expecting this recipe for eggless chocolate chip cookies to be very popular beyond quarantine.

But I was really wrong! It has gone on to be the most popular recipe on my blog, getting over 20 times the views as any other recipe. And I have to admit, it has become one of my favorites too!

Thus, I realized the need for a truly eggless baking cookbook. There are many vegan books out there, but if you can eat butter and dairy, you might be looking for other options. Many dessert recipes are naturally eggless, like many shortbread cookies, but they're not always labeled as *eggless*. As a result, finding eggless dessert recipes can be difficult. In this book, you can count on every recipe to be eggless, and you can easily modify them for your dietary needs. The recipes in this book do call for the use of real butter, milk, dairy, yogurt, and more. But I also give easy substitution advice for people who eat dairy-free or vegan, gluten-free, and nut-free. I also provide baking advice to those of you living at high altitudes.

In *Effortless Eggless Baking* I am going to show you how to bake some of your favorite recipes without eggs. Everything from classic bakes like Cinnamon Rolls (page 58) and Dark Chocolate Fudgy Brownies (page 133) to twists on favorite desserts like Pumpkin Spice Carrot Cake (page 198) and Blueberry Ginger Coffee Cake (page 54). No eggs, no problem! This book is a perfect go-to when you run out of eggs, as the recipes measure up to their egg-filled friends. I use only all-natural and organic ingredients—you'll find no specialty egg replacers here. In fact, the ingredients in these recipes are things you probably already have in your pantry and fridge. I promise you, the bakes in this book will have you wondering why you ever needed eggs in the first place.

BAKING TOOLS

Here you'll find a list of baking tools that I use throughout the book. Most of these tools are essentials that you'll use again and again. Stock your kitchen accordingly so you can bake anytime your craving hits!

BAKING DISHES: For Cinnamon Rolls (page 58) and all the other amazing variations of these fluffy sweet rolls, I use a ceramic 11-by-7-inch baking dish. You can also use an 11-inch ceramic round pie dish for these as well. For all the brownie and bar recipes, I use a 9-by-9-inch baking dish. I prefer to use the USA PAN brand aluminum pans, as they have ridges that really help the brownies rise well.

BAKING SHEETS: A baking sheet (or cookie sheet) might seem like a no-brainer. Maybe you bought one several years ago and it still seems to do the job. But when was the last time you replaced your baking sheets? I know it seems like these run-of-the-mill pans can go and go, but quality aluminum baking sheets really give you better results in your bakes. So think about replacing your old baking sheets. I use aluminum baking sheets because they conduct heat very efficiently.

BOX GRATER: A fine grater is necessary for making Pumpkin Spice Carrot Cake (page 198) or Carrot Zucchini Loaf Cake (page 75). When grating butter for scones you'll want to have a larger grater (think pizza cheese size). This is why I prefer a box grater, as it has four sides with different grater sizes.

CAKE PANS: I use a few different kinds of cake pans for the recipes in this book. The first is a 1-pound loaf pan. This measures at 8.5 by 4.5 by 2.75 inches and is the most common size loaf pan. If you have a 1½-pound loaf pan, you can use that in its place, but just know that your loaf cakes will be wider and shorter. My absolute favorite loaf pans are from USA PAN, as the little ridges in their pans are instrumental for creating perfectly rising cakes. If your loaf cakes aren't rising well, change your pan. When baking without eggs, you want to use the best pans!

For the layer cakes, I use 6-inch cake pans. You'll need three total. I love this size, as it's not so large that it makes a cake you struggle to eat all of, but it's still large enough to share. For coffee cakes, I use a 9-inch pan. For both of these round pans, I use aluminum cake pans. And for the sheet cakes, I use a 9-by-13-inch USA PAN pan. Again, the ridges in these pans really help cakes bake and rise. I highly recommend

investing in some of these pans. They are inexpensive, so they are completely worth it!

CAKE SPINNER: If you are hoping to improve your cake decorating skills, a cake spinner is a must have! This tool helps tremendously in frosting layer cakes because you can spin it as you frost. In commercial baking, a cake spinner is used along with cake rounds, which are cardboard rounds that can be placed on the spinner to keep a cake from sliding around. But for the home baker, cake rounds are not necessary at all. My trick is to add a small dollop of frosting onto the cake spinner, and then add a piece of parchment paper. Place another dollop of frosting onto the parchment paper, put your first cake layer there, and you're good to go! Your finished cake can be easily transferred to a cake dome or cake stand.

CAST-IRON SKILLET: I use a 10-inch cast-iron skillet for the cookie skillet recipes. These are amazing for family dinner dessert: Just top them with ice cream for a sharing dessert that everyone will love. There are many terrific brands of cast-iron skillets out there, such as Staub, Milo, and Le Creuset. A cast-iron skillet is an amazing investment, and you'll have it forever!

CUPCAKE AND MUFFIN PANS AND LINERS: Cupcake and muffin pans can be used interchangeably. I use a USA PAN cupcake pan, but any cupcake pan you have will do. Make sure to have at least two cupcake pans. I prefer to use unbleached cupcake and muffin liners, but any kind you have will work just fine.

DIGITAL FOOD SCALE: I can't stress enough how important having a digital food scale is! This is a very inexpensive tool that will only enhance your baking. You can buy a scale for as little as $10 on Amazon. The brand is not important, just that it has a grams mode. You can find small ones that will fit inside a kitchen drawer. If you measure your ingredients on a scale, you can take the guesswork out of baking and confirm that you're measuring properly. This is my number one tip for home bakers: Buy a scale and get familiar with using it. Plus, it doesn't create as many dishes to wash—you gotta love that!

DRINK THERMOMETER: A drink thermometer will help when you're heating liquids. This is important for working with ingredients such as milk, which is in Earl Grey Lemon Loaf Cake (page 78). Milk should be heated to only 140 to 160°F; going above 160°F will burn the milk. That burnt flavor will transfer into your baked goods, and you definitely don't want that.

FOOD PROCESSOR: A food processor is a great tool to have! I use it to make graham cracker crusts for tarts and for making cakes such as my Blueberry Pistachio Loaf Cake (page 87). A small food processor, such as a 3-cup size, will work for these recipes.

KITCHEN TORCH: A kitchen torch is an inexpensive kitchen tool that is a luxurious necessity, in my opinion. It is so fun to torch desserts! You'll want to have one for torching the Peanut Butter S'More Tart (page 178). Try it: I'm sure it will become a favorite recipe. (Even if you don't have a kitchen torch, this recipe is still delicious!)

KNIVES: It's good to have a sharp knife for chopping nuts or chocolate, and for cutting biscotti. I prefer to use a chef's knife over a serrated knife for biscotti. Regardless, one good chef's knife will work for all the recipes here.

MEASURING CUPS AND SPOONS: While I do recommend measuring all your dry ingredients with a digital food scale, you will need measuring cups and spoons for some of the other ingredients. Measuring cups are needed for milk, cream, lemon juice, and more. And you'll need measuring spoons for important ingredients like vanilla extract, salt, baking soda, and more.

MIXING BOWLS: It's good to have a few medium to large mixing bowls. These can be metal, glass, or plastic if you're using them to just measure ingredients on the scale. I also recommend that you have at least one heatproof bowl for melting chocolate. That heatproof bowl can be metal or glass, but I prefer to use metal for melting chocolate in a double boiler.

OVEN THERMOMETER: While your oven may be the most obvious tool in your kitchen, it can be overlooked as a tool in and of itself. You might think as long as it turns on, it works. But it's important to know if your oven is baking at the right temperature because if it isn't, it could be the very tool keeping you from baked-good perfection.

If you have an electric oven, the bake times noted in this book should be very accurate. If you have a gas oven, you may find some recipes take a few minutes longer to bake all the way through. For this reason, I provide a time range that you can expect to stay within, as well as visual cues to look for doneness. Be sure to look for the visual signs that your baked goods are done—don't just rely on the time. Every single oven is going to be a little different, so take some time to get to know your oven and you'll end up being better friends!

Getting an oven thermometer is a great investment, no matter if your oven is old or brand new (inconsistent oven temperatures don't discriminate!). Oven thermometers are inexpensive, usually costing around $10. You can pop it in now and then to double-check that your oven is heating properly, or you can leave it in all the time for extra precision! I leave mine in at all times and glance at it before baking anything. If you notice it's reading a different temperature than what your oven says, you can either call a repair guy to fix the oven or adjust the oven temperature to get it just right.

PARCHMENT PAPER: I use parchment paper for everything! As I've found during my commercial baking experience, it truly helps remove cakes from pans much more efficiently. You can do without, however, as it's not required for most recipes. But if you are not using parchment paper, be sure to grease pans very well. Parchment paper just makes baking easier, I think! My favorite brand is Kana; their parchment paper sheets are responsibly made and completely compostable and biodegradable. You can also easily find reusable unbleached parchment paper on Amazon, which would be the next best option.

PASTRY BRUSH: A pastry brush is super important for putting Pie Wash (page 163) on any of the pies made from the recipes in this book. Traditional pies usually have an egg wash, but don't worry: I've got you covered with plenty of other options for making that pie crust golden brown! I prefer to use a silicone pastry brush, simply because I think they are easier to clean. But a traditional pastry brush will work just as well.

PIE AND TART PANS: You need only two pans to make all the pie and tart recipes in this book. For pies I use a standard 9-inch pie dish. I prefer to use an aluminum pie pan as opposed to glass or ceramic, as it yields the best results for baking pies and doesn't leave the bottom of the crust soggy. Especially at high altitude, this is key! My favorite pie pan is the USA PAN pie pan, as the little ridges really help to bake the best pies, especially the crust. Ceramic or glass will work, but you may need to bake pies a little bit longer. For the tarts, I use a 9½-inch tart pan. It is important to have a true tart pan, where the bottom removes easily, because it allows you to get your tart out in perfect shape. For this reason, avoid using a ceramic tart pan that doesn't have the removable bottom.

PIE WEIGHTS: Pie weights are used when you need to parbake (which stands for partially bake) a pie crust before filling it. Parbaking needs to be done when baking Pecan Pie (page 190). Commercial pie weights are fancy and can be used, but they are not necessary at all. Because parchment paper is put down on top of the pie dough before parbaking, you can also use rice, beans, or quinoa as weight on the pie dough before parbaking. I have a tub in my pantry with rice labeled PIE WEIGHTS that I use again and again for my "pie weights." A few cups of rice or beans are much cheaper than a set of commercial pie weights, and you can reuse them over and over again!

PIPING BAGS AND PIPING TIPS: Piping bags and tips are not necessary for frosting cupcakes, as you can easily apply frosting with just a butter knife or spatula. But they do make them look pretty, and they make the job much easier! I recommend purchasing 16- to 18-inch piping bags, as that will fit the amount of frosting for a recipe of cupcakes. I use the Ateco piping tips #808, #827, #846, and #864. You can purchase a variety of Ateco tips together in a pack.

POT: I use a small saucepan as a double boiler along with a heatproof bowl for melting chocolate. A 2-quart pot will work just fine.

SIFTER: A sifter is necessary for any recipe calling for powdered sugar or cocoa. Both of these ingredients are known for clumping very easily, especially if they've been in the pantry for even just a few weeks! So sifting is key for texture in your final baked goods. I prefer the old-school-style sifters that are stainless steel with the hand crank. I'd recommend purchasing a 3-cup sifter. If you don't have a sifter, a fine mesh strainer will work in its place as long as you're willing to get your hands dirty!

SPATULAS: You should have a couple good rubber spatulas for stirring cake batter and frosting cakes. I use a cake spatula for finishing layer cakes, which also comes in handy for smoothing the tops of sheet cakes.

STAND MIXER: A stand mixer is an especially helpful tool for your kitchen. Most of the recipes in this book call for a stand mixer with a paddle attachment. A whisk attachment is also needed to make whipped cream. I use a dough hook to make Cinnamon Rolls (page 58) and Chocolate Pecan Babka (page 91).

If you don't have a stand mixer, you can use a couple different tools in its place. Whenever a recipe calls for a stand mixer with a paddle attachment, you can substitute a bowl with a wooden spoon or spatula—just be ready for an arm workout. In place of a stand mixer with a whisk attachment, you can use a hand mixer. And in place of the stand mixer with a dough hook, you can use your hands! The stand mixer will just make mixing easier for you, but it is not necessary. I love them because they are hands-free, allowing me to do other things while my whipped cream whips up or my cinnamon roll dough is kneading.

TIMER: A timer is key for making any baked good! Make sure to have a kitchen timer. Even the timer on your phone will do.

EGG-FREE ESSENTIALS

What do eggs do? Before we bake without eggs, we need to know what eggs bring to baked goods so they can be properly replaced. Eggs are a staple in many desserts because they aren't just a one-hit wonder. Eggs bring fat, flavor, structure, moisture, and fluffiness. They can even act as a glaze, such as on top of a pie.

Now you may be thinking . . . fat, flavor, structure, moisture, and *fluffiness*—I need all of that in my baked goods! How could I ever bake without eggs? It's all about replacing the eggs with something that can act in a similar way. For example, in my recipe for Chocolate Chip Cookies (page 95), I replace eggs with whole milk. This provides flavor, fat, and moisture—three things that eggs provide in a typical chocolate chip cookie recipe.

I'll let you in on a little secret: Eggs can actually make baked goods dry out faster than baked goods without eggs. Why? Because egg whites are mostly water and not fat, and water tends to have a drying effect on baked goods. When you use whole eggs in baked goods, you're including extra water via those egg whites. So, if you're going to leave your cookies out at a party, my eggless Chocolate Chip Cookies (page 95) actually fare better than cookies with eggs! Plus, they're so good no one will even know the difference.

Aside from whole milk, you can use plenty of other ingredients to mimic the benefits of eggs in your baked goods. Here are some common ingredients I use for this purpose. I recommend having them on hand in your kitchen.

APPLESAUCE: I love using applesauce, as it has an amazing texture and a pretty neutral flavor, mostly adding a little sweetness that is perfect for any dessert. Applesauce brings moisture, flavor, and even structure to baked goods. I use organic applesauce, and any brand you find will work just fine.

AQUAFABA: This may be the most unique ingredient in the book, and it's only used in a couple recipes. So, if you don't have it, no worries! Aquafaba is made from the liquid of boiled chickpeas. Yes, chickpeas! This comes in a powder form, meaning you can easily stock your pantry with it. You just mix the powder with water and use the liquid in recipes. It's a natural ingredient that can be whisked to create a similar texture to egg whites. I use Vör Aquafaba Powder in the few recipes in this book that call for it.

BAKING POWDER AND BAKING SODA: These are common leavening agents used in all baked goods. They are especially helpful for baked goods without eggs, as eggs can help sweets rise naturally. I use aluminum-free baking powder and soda. My favorite is Frontier Co-Op, which can be purchased in bulk from their website. Both of these leavening agents should be kept in a cool dry place, and they will last about six months once opened. If you're unsure when you last purchased your baking powder or soda, replace it before baking so that you can be sure it will work!

BUTTER: Butter is one of my all-time favorite ingredients. When it's whipped, butter can be used to help replace the fluffiness of eggs. Butter can also be used as a browning agent, such as for a glaze on top of a pie, which will add extra flavor. I always use salted butter, as it has more flavor. Plus, if I'm baking or cooking, I don't need to worry about swapping out butter. My favorite brand is Organic Valley, but there are many out there that will also work just as well. If you are using unsalted butter, just make sure to add ¼ teaspoon of salt for every ½ cup of unsalted butter. Vegan butter can be substituted, but try to use a stick version like Miyoko's Creamery European-Style Cultured Vegan Butter with a Hint of Sea Salt.

CORNSTARCH: Eggs can be used to make custard and tarts because they create their own structure. For the same reason, cornstarch can be used in place of eggs for certain fillings, like in Pecan Pie (page 190), because it's a thickening agent. Cornstarch is also used in pies to thicken fruit juices and keep them from leaking out of the crust. I prefer to buy organic cornstarch, and my favorite brand is Frontier Co-Op.

HEAVY WHIPPING CREAM: Heavy whipping cream is similar to milk, as it can be used for fat, flavor, and moisture. I tend to use heavy whipping cream over milk if I want even more moisture or a velvety-smooth texture, like in a chocolate cake. It can also be used on top of pie to create a golden brown pie crust. My favorite kind is Organic Valley, but many others out there are just as good! You can also substitute full-fat canned coconut cream in its place if you don't want to use dairy.

MILK: I often use milk to replace eggs and bring moisture and fat to a dessert. That's why using whole milk is very important. There are some recipes where I use chocolate milk because it can add even more flavor to already-chocolaty desserts. However, chocolate milk can always be replaced with regular whole milk. If you are trying to avoid dairy, then substituting a full-fat coconut milk is the next best option. My favorite coconut milk is So Delicious Unsweetened Vanilla Coconut Milk, and it can be used in place of milk in any recipe in this book.

SOUR CREAM: I like to use sour cream when I need fat as well as structure. Sour cream can act as a binder and hold things together a little more than milk or cream. It provides fat and flavor too. If your sour cream is really thin (I find Straus is always too thin), swap it out for another brand that is thicker, like Organic Valley or Humboldt Creamery. You can also use a nondairy sour cream; my favorite option is Forager Project Organic Dairy-Free Sour Cream.

YOGURT: I love using yogurt for flavor and structure. I always use full-fat vanilla yogurt. You can also use full-fat plain if you prefer, but the vanilla gives it a little sweetness that I like. Don't use low-fat or fat-free yogurt. There are also dairy-free yogurts you can use in place as well; my favorites are the coconut- or cashew-based ones, as they have the best flavor for desserts.

OTHER PANTRY INGREDIENTS

ALL-PURPOSE FLOUR: Organic all-purpose flour is used most commonly throughout this book. Any brand you like will be just fine, as they are all fairly similar. Just make sure to get an organic unbleached all-purpose flour, as that is the best kind! I always prefer to use organic ingredients, as they will actually bring more flavor to baked goods because they are not as processed. This is also why I choose unbleached all-purpose flour. Organic unbleached all-purpose flour does not cost much more than traditional flour. It's an easy switch to make that will make a big difference in your baked goods. Even a grocery store brand will work! As a reminder, all flours weigh a little differently. So, for the best results, make sure to use a scale when measuring flour.

BROWN SUGARS: I use both dark brown and light brown sugar for the recipes in this book. They can be interchangeable, so if you have only one on hand and you're in a pinch, go ahead and use it. The texture of the final product won't be affected, but the same can't be said for the taste. Dark brown sugar is, well, darker than light brown sugar, and the darker the color the more flavor it has. That flavor builds into the flavors of the recipe. In other words, if you use light brown in place of dark brown, the flavor will be lighter and less rich. My favorite brands are Florida Crystals and Wholesome. But, truth be told, most brands will be very similar. If you're not going through your brown sugar quickly, be sure to store it in an airtight container so it doesn't dry out.

CAKE FLOUR: Cake flour is key for cakes, cupcakes, and loaf cakes. My favorite brand for cake flour is King Arthur, as there isn't an organic option on the market yet and this is non-GMO. This is the cake flour I use at home and what I used to bake all the recipes in this book!

CANE SUGAR: Cane sugar is the organic equivalent of granulated white sugar. They work the same in recipes; they just don't look the same or taste the same. Organic cane sugar is a little bit darker than granulated—it's not quite white but more of a tan color. It also has larger crystals because it hasn't been processed like granulated sugar. Any brand of organic cane sugar will do! If you substitute granulated white sugar, just keep in mind the final products won't look exactly like the photos in this book, as they will be much lighter in color.

CANOLA OIL: I feel like canola oil has gotten a bad rap over the years. So let me remind you that if you are using organic canola oil, then you're not harming the environment and you're not consuming GMOs. All the more reason to buy organic! I like using canola oil, as it has a very neutral flavor. Sometimes that's exactly what you need for certain recipes. You can always substitute melted coconut oil for canola oil in any recipe, if you prefer.

CANOLA OIL COOKING SPRAY: This ingredient is a luxury to have, but it's one that I find incredibly helpful. I always buy organic. Your local grocery store will probably have this spray in the baking aisle. I use this spray for greasing muffin pans so the large tops won't stick. I also use it to grease the bowl of sweet roll dough, as it's quick, easy, and works so well!

CHOCOLATE: I use all kinds of chocolate for the recipes in this book—dark chocolate, milk chocolate, semisweet chocolate, and white chocolate. All of which I buy organic. My favorite place to buy chocolate for baking is Mama Ganache; which you can purchase in bulk from their website.

COCONUT: The best coconut is unsweetened, always. Never buy the sweetened stuff, as it's full of unnecessary additives and actually tastes less like coconut! I use only one type of coconut for the recipes in this book, and that's unsweetened fine shredded coconut. You can find this at most health food stores, sometimes even in the bulk section. Or you can find it online from retailers like Amazon.

COCONUT FLOUR: I use coconut flour in a handful of recipes in this book. My favorite organic coconut flour is made by Bob's Red Mill, but many other brands will be just as good. I use coconut flour to help dry out desserts and add flavor. Because coconut flour is so specific, do not substitute it for anything else, as other flours do not act the same way.

COCONUT MILK: I use coconut milk in a few recipes where I want the flavor to shine through, like Chocolate Coconut Bars (page 144). You can use coconut milk in place of milk in any recipe. My favorite is So Delicious Unsweetened Vanilla Coconut Milk.

COCONUT OIL: I love using coconut oil in desserts because it provides a slightly coconut taste. As someone who loves coconut, I love that! But if you are sensitive to coconut flavor, you can substitute canola oil for melted coconut oil in any recipe. You can also get a refined coconut oil, which has had the coconut flavor removed. Either type of coconut oil you purchase will work the same.

CREAM CHEESE: Cream cheese is essential for Rainbow Fruit Cheesecake Tart (page 180). That tart is so good, you'll definitely want to make that in the summer months. Make sure to use a full-fat cream cheese. My favorite brand is Organic Valley, but there are others out there that will work just as well.

DUTCH COCOA POWDER: I prefer to use Dutch cocoa powder in all my recipes. Dutch-processed cocoa powder has a smoother and richer flavor than natural cocoa powder. If you have natural cocoa powder and prefer to use it, you can use that in its place, but your baked goods may not be as dark in color or as rich in flavor when using natural cocoa powder.

FLAVORS AND EXTRACTS: Flavors and extracts are key for making baked goods pop with flavor. Vanilla extract is a staple and is used in about half of the recipes in this book! My favorite brand of vanilla extract is Simply Organic. You can find this at most grocery stores and health food stores. I also use a few organic flavors for the recipes in this book, such as almond extract, lemon flavor, orange flavor, and peppermint flavor. I buy the Frontier Co-Op brand for these, as I find they have the most true flavors. The best thing about Frontier Co-Op is they are an actual co-op, and you can sign up and order online! They also own Simply Organic, so you can get all your flavors and extracts in one place. As for coconut extract, I prefer the brand Flavorganics.

These are the flavors I like. You may find you like other brands, but the most important part is that you find the flavors and extracts you enjoy. There are many different options for the same flavor! If you use one you don't like, don't give up on the recipe because of that—not all flavors and extracts are good. This is why it's important to spend a little extra here and buy the good stuff.

It's important to know that flavors and extracts cannot be substituted for fresh lemon or orange juice. Flavors and extracts are a concentrated flavor, which is why they are so important in baking. Flavors and extracts can provide the amount of flavor needed without drastically altering the liquid in a recipe. The amount of fresh lemon juice you'd need to match 1 teaspoon of lemon flavor would alter some recipes too much and it wouldn't bake properly.

Also, flavors and extracts are not interchangeable. Extracts are more concentrated, and flavors are less concentrated. If you are swapping one for the other, such as almond flavor for almond extract, make sure to use this ratio:

1 teaspoon extract = 2 teaspoons flavor

GLUTEN-FREE FLOUR: Most of the recipes in this book have gluten-free variations. Look for them down at the bottom of a recipe. The best gluten-free flour (in my opinion), and what the recipes were tested with, is Namaste Organic Perfect Flour Blend. You can try to use other gluten-free flours in these recipes, but make sure to use a blend and not just a single type. All flours weigh and measure a little differently, so if you are using a different brand of gluten-free flour, for the best results make sure to weigh it. You can find the Namaste brand on Amazon and at many health food stores.

GRAHAM CRACKERS: I use graham crackers when making crusts for tarts. My favorite is Annie's Organic Honey Graham Crackers, but even your grocery store brand of organic honey grahams will work! If you are using gluten-free graham crackers, be sure to weigh them! Many gluten-free graham crackers come in sizes that differ from traditional ones, so using the sleeve measurements could provide you with the wrong amount. This is a good example why weighing ingredients is important for baking.

GROUND VANILLA BEAN: I like to use organic ground vanilla bean in baking because it provides a different vanilla flavor than vanilla extract. It is actually a stronger and more intense flavor, as the beans are more potent. If you do not have ground vanilla bean, you may use this ratio to substitute vanilla extract:

  1 teaspoon ground vanilla bean =
  2 teaspoons vanilla extract

KAMUT FLOUR: I use this specialty flour in Chocolate-Dipped Shortbreads (page 115) because it's truly necessary to get the flavor of these amazing cookies! My favorite brand is Food to Live. In my opinion, they produce the best kamut flour with the best flavor.

MAPLE SYRUP: I love using maple syrup as a sweetener. It adds so much amazing flavor to desserts! Always buy pure organic maple syrup. And I prefer to buy a darker color syrup (formerly known as Grade B), as it has a more true maple flavor.

NUT BUTTERS: Peanut butter is one of my favorite ingredients to use in eggless baking, as it not only has amazing flavor, but its structure is very helpful. I prefer to use smooth peanut butter that is organic, of course. I like to buy organic peanut butter that only has two ingredients: dry roasted peanuts and sea salt. My two favorite brands are Smucker's and Kirkland (yes, from Costco!). I also use organic varieties of cashew butter and almond butter. All the nut butters are interchangeable, so if you want to use peanut butter in place of almond butter or cashew butter in place of almond butter, that's just fine!

NUTS: There are many nuts used throughout the recipes in this book. I stick to organic nuts all the time. You should be able to find most everything at your local grocery store. Make sure to check the recipe to see if it says roasted and salted or not. If not, then raw nuts are just fine! But when a recipe calls for roasted and salted, know that the nuts will be providing flavor and salt, so make sure to use that type.

POWDERED SUGAR: Powdered sugar is also known as confectioners' sugar. They are the same. I just prefer to call it *powdered sugar,* as it's how I was introduced to it. There is always some sort of starch in powdered sugar to keep it from caking. I have a tapioca allergy, so I use the Florida Crystals brand because it uses cornstarch. The Wholesome brand, by contrast, uses tapioca starch. Both of these organic brands are great, and they work the same. Powdered sugar will clump if it sits in the pantry for a while. Just make sure to sift it for all recipes!

SALT: Salt is a very important ingredient in baking! I use a fine sea salt for baked goods all the time, as I feel it has the best flavor. I buy it from Frontier Co-Op in bulk. I sometimes use a coarse sea salt for topping. This is always optional, and you can always substitute fine sea salt in its place. I just like the texture and look of coarse sea salt for a finishing salt.

SPICES: I use Frontier Co-Op for all my spices. I love purchasing from them because I can buy in bulk. I purchase 1-pound bags of spices and then stock my own spice jars. It saves on waste because I'm not throwing away the jar every single time, as would be the case if I purchased it directly from the grocery store. And because I like to have larger spice jars than the typical grocery store size, I buy bigger jars and fill them myself.

SPRINKLES: Rainbow sprinkles are something that are never needed but are always wanted. Any recipe would be okay without sprinkles, but it wouldn't be as fun! I always use rainbow sprinkles without artificial colors. My favorite brand is India Tree Nature's Colors Carnival Mix sprinkles because I love the pastel look. They have a vegan option as well! Sprinkles from India Tree are what I use throughout the book. You can also use ColorKitchen Rainbow Sprinkles if you are looking for a brighter and more vibrant color. Both brands make their sprinkles using plant-based dyes with very similar ingredients. Both are easily available on Amazon!

EASY SUBSTITUTIONS

Most all of my recipes are designed to make easy substitutions. Here I've listed some typical substitutions you may want to try out if you have allergies or dietary restrictions, along with some tips and tricks for each. And if you live at high altitude, I got you covered!

Gluten-Free

I know many people are gluten-free, and I provide gluten-free substitutions for most of the recipes in this book. I highly recommend using the gluten-free flour blend I note in the Other Pantry Ingredients section, Namaste Organic Perfect Flour Blend. This is what I used when testing the recipes in this book. All gluten-free flours are a little different, and I've found this one has the best structure to mimic wheat as well as the best flavor and texture.

Whenever making a cookie dough or cake batter, the gluten-free version will always seem a little more sticky or thick—this is normal! When scooping gluten-free cookie dough, be sure to flatten the cookies a little bit more than the recipe notes, as gluten-free flour doesn't rise or spread as much as wheat flour. If you don't follow this extra step, your cookies may seem smaller and thicker. Your cakes may also be shorter, as gluten-free flour doesn't rise like wheat flour. If you are going to try an alternative gluten-free flour from the one I recommend, be sure to use a gluten-free flour blend as opposed to rice, almond, or coconut flours. These flours alone will not give you the same results. As always, for accuracy be sure to measure your flour by weight and not by cups.

Vegan and Dairy-Free

If you eat dairy-free or vegan, the good news is you can substitute the dairy in my recipes for nondairy versions.

In place of whole milk, use coconut milk. This is the best milk substitute, as it still has fat and flavor, which is very important for baking. My favorite is So Delicious Unsweetened Vanilla Coconut Milk.

In place of heavy whipping cream, you can substitute full-fat coconut cream from a can. Just be sure to stir the coconut cream completely when you open the can, as it usually has cream on top—and when substituting coconut cream for heavy whipping cream, you want to make sure it's stirred well to mimic the same consistency as traditional cream.

You can also replace butter with a vegan butter. My top pick is Miyoko's Creamery

European-Style Cultured Vegan Butter with a Hint of Sea Salt. It comes in sticks and tastes amazing. Vegan butter that comes in sticks is always better for baking than vegan butter from a tub. The consistency of the sticks is a little different, providing more structure and making it easier to measure. The Miyoko's sticks do contain cashews, so if you have a nut allergy, then the Miyoko's Creamery Spreadable Cultured Vegan Oat Milk Butter is the next best thing. It works especially well in cookies. For frostings, pies, and cakes I would highly recommend another vegan butter stick like Earth Balance Vegan Buttery Sticks.

For other dairy ingredients such as cream cheese and sour cream, my favorite brand is Forager Project, as they offer organic products. You can also use plant-based meat substitutes for the few savory recipes, such as Ham, Cheese & Chives Scones (page 41). And you can use an organic coconut bacon, such as from Madly Hadley, for the Maple Bacon Scones (page 49).

Nut-Free

If you eat nut-free, try substituting a sunflower seed butter for recipes that call for peanut butter, cashew butter, or almond butter. If you see nuts in a recipe, like in the Chocolate Pecan Babka (page 91), you can simply omit them—or even add chocolate chips in their place!

High-Altitude

All of my recipes are tested at high altitude and sea level, meaning you can bake these recipes no matter where you live. Each recipe is written for sea level, and at the bottom there's a note for making a high-altitude adjustment. So, if you live at 5,000 feet or higher, make sure to check the note at the bottom for the baking time that will work best for you. As always, make sure to look for visual signs that your

baked goods are done before taking them out of the oven.

STORAGE INSTRUCTIONS

Baking is a thing all its own, but storing your baked goods is just as important as actually baking them! Because what good are they if you can't enjoy them for days to come? I'm going to break down the desserts in this book for you here and give you the best storage instructions for making your baked goods last. My first tip: Foil is not a suitable cover for anything! Foil may seem fine, but it's never truly airtight, so your baked goods will always suffer and begin to dry out. Alternatively, adding foil over something that should be out in the open air will trap moisture and compromise its flaky or crispy texture.

Muffins and Cupcakes

These are best stored at room temperature in an airtight container for up to 3 days. No one likes a dry muffin or cupcake. This is why the airtight container is super important. It keeps the cake moist, as the liner doesn't do enough on its own! The best airtight containers are glass or plastic with sealable lids, zip-lock sealable bags, and my favorite, a cake dome. If you don't have a cake dome, I highly recommend getting one. You can use it for so many things, and it's a great way to display baked goods while keeping them fresh.

Sweet Rolls and Coffee Cakes

These are best when eaten right away, in my opinion. But if you are storing them, then a cake dome is your absolute best option. As these recipes produce large final products, you'd have to cut them up or dismantle them in order to get them into a small container or bag, so a cake dome is really the best! They'll keep for up to 3 days.

Scones

Scone are actually best kept out in the open air. You can leave them out on the counter on a plate for up to 3 days. I wouldn't recommend putting them in a cake dome, as they can actually get soggy in there.

Loaf Cakes

The best way to store loaf cakes is to cut them up (I usually get about eight slices per loaf) and wrap each slice in plastic wrap. I don't usually like using plastic wrap, but if you stack all the loaf slices in a sealable container, they will most likely stick together because they are moist cakes. In addition, if you wrap them individually, you can just grab one to take with you! They will keep for up to 3 days.

Soft Cookies and Cookie Pies

These are best kept in an airtight container of any kind. You can use zip-lock sealable bags, glass or plastic containers, or even a cake dome. They'll stay good for up to 7 days as long as they are in an airtight container. You can also freeze them for up to 1 month too! Throw your sealed containers or zip-lock plastic bags right into the freezer and pull out the cookies whenever you want them. The best thing about this type of cookie is that they thaw out in minutes!

Shortbread Cookies, Sandwich Cookies, and Thumbprints

Because shortbreads are buttery, crisp, and sweet, they should not be stored in an airtight container. They are best when left out in the open and have access to air, as it helps them keep their texture. These are perfect for adding to an old-fashioned cookie jar, one that doesn't have an airtight seal. Or you can leave them on a plate on the counter for up to 7 days. Or you can freeze them for up to 1 month! If you are freezing them, you should put them in a sealed glass or plastic container or a zip-lock plastic bag.

Brownies and Bars

These are best stored in an airtight container. I always cut my brownies or bars as soon as they've cooled, and I put them in a sealed glass or plastic container. Putting them into zip-lock sealable bags or individually wrapping them in plastic wrap also works! Brownies and bars will last up to 5 days at room temperature, or you can freeze them for up to 1 month. Just be sure they are wrapped up well in an airtight container for the freezer. Bars that have frosting on top, like Gingerbread Bars (page 149), are best if you individually wrap them in plastic wrap. If you stack them in a glass or plastic container, the frosting from one will stick to another.

Biscotti

Very similar to shortbreads, biscotti are supposed to be crisp. For this reason they should not be stored in an airtight container. They are best when left out in the open and have access to air, as it helps them keep their texture. These are perfect for adding to a cookie jar that doesn't have an airtight seal, like an old-fashioned cookie jar. Or you can leave them on a plate on the counter for up to 7 days. Or you can freeze them for up to 1 month! If you are freezing them, you should put them in a sealed glass or plastic container or a zip-lock plastic bag.

Cakes

Layer cakes and sheet cakes should be stored in an airtight container so the cake stays moist. If you have a cake dome, you're in luck—a 6-inch layer cake usually fits perfectly inside one. Sheet cakes are a little more tricky, as they are baked in a 9-by-13-inch pan. You can wrap the pan with plastic wrap to keep it airtight, or you can cut up the slices and add them to a sealed glass or plastic container. I usually do the latter, as then the slices are already cut and it's easy to pull one out of the container when I want it. Cake is good for up to 3 days if stored in an airtight container.

Cake Balls

These guys are pretty durable, as the cake is sealed inside a chocolate coating. You can leave these at room temperature, in the fridge, or even freeze them! I actually keep all my cake balls in the freezer, as then I can just pull a couple out when I want them. That way I don't feel the need to eat them all immediately after I make them. I store them in an airtight container before freezing. They will stay good at room temperature or in the fridge for up to 3 days, or in the freezer for up to 1 month.

Fruit Pies, Hand Pies, and Toaster Pastries

These are best kept at room temperature, as we want to keep that pie crust flaky. Pies will stay good for up to 3 days at room temperature, with no covering. Don't cover them up in a dome or even put them in an airtight container, as that will make the flaky crust become soggy.

Cheesecake Tarts and Whipped Cream Frosting Desserts

These are best eaten right away. Homemade whipped cream, whether it's whipped into a filling or added on top, doesn't have stabilizers like the store-bought kind, so it begins to deflate soon after it's made. This deflation will happen gradually over a couple days. If you must store them, wrap with plastic wrap and keep them in the fridge for no longer than 3 days.

PRO TIP: If you live in a very humid climate or are experiencing very humid weather, crispy and flaky desserts will become soft incredibly faster than usual. In this case, the fridge can sometimes be the best storage choice. Or you can just eat your desserts and share them with friends and neighbors!

Breakfast Bakes

There's nothing like a freshly baked breakfast. The recipes in this chapter are perfect for a leisurely morning. Muffins take less time, while scones and cinnamon rolls take a little more. And if you're hosting Sunday brunch, you can make up an entire menu with recipes out of this chapter alone. Traditional bakes like Cinnamon Rolls (page 58) and Blueberry Muffins (page 27) will fill those nostalgic cravings you may have had for some time, as most recipes for these bakes usually contain eggs.

Also look for nontraditional brunch recipes, like Chocolate Peanut Butter Honey Sweet Rolls (page 60), Cheddar Jalapeño Scones (page 45), and my favorite of the whole brunch (pun intended)—Blueberry Ginger Coffee Cake (page 54)! When I get to have a leisurely morning to take the time to bake something amazing for breakfast, it's truly a treat.

    If you're looking to bake ahead for a special occasion like Christmas morning, try my Cinnamon Swirl Coffee Cake (page 57), as this recipe will stay fresh sealed in the cake pan overnight thanks to the crumble topping covering it. Simply remove from the pan and serve in the morning. You can also prep any of these sweet roll recipes the day before, down to cutting the rolls and placing them in the baking dish. Then just cover the baking dish with plastic wrap and store it in the fridge overnight. Remove the baking dish from the fridge while the oven is preheating and bake them. The result is freshly baked sweet rolls any day you want.

BLUEBERRY MUFFINS

MAKES 12 MUFFINS

Blueberry muffins are a classic breakfast bake. I like to use yogurt and heavy whipping cream for structure and moisture to mimic the eggs in these muffins. A tip for getting that large iconic muffin top to remove easily from the pan is to spray the entire muffin tin with a canola oil cooking spray before scooping. This helps to easily remove them without them sticking or breaking after they have puffed up and come over the tops.

2 cups (255 g) all-purpose flour

¾ cup (170 g) cane sugar, plus extra for topping

2 teaspoons baking powder

½ teaspoon cinnamon

½ teaspoon fine sea salt

½ cup (113 g) salted butter, cold

1 cup (237 ml) heavy whipping cream

½ cup (113 g) vanilla yogurt

1 teaspoon vanilla extract

6 ounces (170 g) blueberries

Preheat the oven to 350°F. Line a muffin tin with liners.

In the bowl of a stand mixer fitted with the paddle attachment, add the flour, cane sugar, baking powder, cinnamon, and sea salt and swirl together.

Using a large grater, grate the butter into the mixing bowl. Add the whipping cream, yogurt, and vanilla extract and mix on low until combined into a stiff batter.

Fold in the blueberries with a spatula. Fill the cupcake liners full and sprinkle the tops with cane sugar.

Bake for 25 to 30 minutes, until a toothpick inserted in the center comes out clean.

Store in an airtight container for up to 3 days.

GLUTEN-FREE

Replace the all-purpose flour with 1⅔ cups (255 g) gluten-free flour blend.

HIGH ALTITUDE

Bake at 350°F for 20 to 25 minutes, until a toothpick inserted in the center comes out clean.

MAPLE-GLAZED BANANA CHOCOLATE CHIP MUFFINS

MAKES 14 MUFFINS

I'm sure you all know that when baking banana breads, cakes, or muffins, you should use very ripe, browning bananas. But you may not know exactly why. As the bananas start to ripen (and turn brown), the starches in the banana turn into sugars. This gives these bananas more banana flavor and more sweetness. Plus they are also easier to mix and incorporate into batters without chunks. All the more reason to use your extra-ripe bananas! Bananas are also a great egg replacer. I don't like to use them for everything, as the banana flavor shines through. But in banana desserts they are the perfect ingredient!

BATTER

- ½ cup (113 g) salted butter, softened
- ½ cup (113 g) packed dark brown sugar
- ¼ cup (57 g) cane sugar
- 2 large ripe bananas
- ½ cup (118 ml) heavy whipping cream, room temperature
- ¼ cup (57 g) sour cream, room temperature
- 2 cups (284 g) cake flour, plus 2 teaspoons for coating
- ¾ teaspoon baking powder
- ½ teaspoon fine sea salt
- ½ teaspoon cinnamon
- ½ cup (99 g) semisweet chocolate chips

GLAZE

- ½ cup (71 g) powdered sugar, sifted
- 3 tablespoons (66 g) maple syrup

Preheat the oven to 350°F. Line a muffin pan with liners.

TO MAKE THE BATTER: In the bowl of a stand mixer fitted with the paddle attachment, add the butter, brown sugar, and cane sugar. Mix on low until combined and there are no chunks of butter.

Add the bananas, whipping cream, and sour cream and mix on low until combined, scrape the sides of the bowl down, and mix again.

Add the 2 cups of cake flour, baking powder, sea salt, and cinnamon in that order. Mix on low until combined, scraping down the sides of the bowl as needed.

In a separate bowl, add the chocolate chips and sprinkle the 2 teaspoons of cake flour on top. Mix to coat them completely. Add the chocolate chips to the batter and fold to combine completely. Fill the muffin liners full with batter.

Bake for 25 to 30 minutes, until a toothpick inserted in the center comes out clean. Allow to cool completely in the muffin pan.

TO MAKE THE GLAZE: In a medium bowl, add the powdered sugar and maple syrup and whisk together until you have a smooth glaze. Drizzle over the tops of the muffins.

Store in an airtight container for up to 3 days.

GLUTEN-FREE

Replace the cake flour with 1¾ cups plus 1½ tablespoons (284 g) gluten-free flour blend.

HIGH ALTITUDE

Bake at 350°F for 20 to 25 minutes, until a toothpick inserted in the center comes out clean.

CHOCOLATE COCONUT ZUCCHINI MUFFINS

MAKES 12 MUFFINS

Before I lived in Mammoth Lakes, California, I would visit my friend Anita there and stay with her family. Her mom was the sweetest woman ever, and she always made sure we had food, snacks, and dessert *at all times*. She baked a chocolate zucchini cake that I will forever be in love with, and it is what turned me on to the combination of chocolate and zucchini. I love using zucchini in muffins and cakes, as it makes a very moist and delicate cake sans eggs. The combination of the light cake with chocolate makes for a truly amazing muffin that is perfect for any brunch spread.

1½ cups (191 g) all-purpose flour

⅓ cup (28 g) fine shredded unsweetened coconut, plus extra for topping

⅓ cup (28 g) Dutch cocoa powder, sifted

¾ teaspoon baking powder

½ teaspoon fine sea salt

¼ teaspoon ginger

6 ounces (170 g) finely grated zucchini

½ cup (118 ml) canola oil

½ cup (113 g) packed dark brown sugar

½ cup (113 g) cane sugar

½ cup (118 ml) milk

Preheat the oven to 350°F. Line a muffin pan with liners.

In the bowl of a stand mixer fitted with the paddle attachment, add the flour, coconut, cocoa, baking powder, sea salt, and ginger and mix for two to three rotations to combine the dry ingredients.

Add the zucchini, canola oil, brown sugar, cane sugar, and milk and mix on low until combined. Fill the cupcake liners full and sprinkle with coconut.

Bake for 25 to 30 minutes, until a toothpick inserted in the center comes out clean. Allow to cool completely in the muffin pan.

Store in an airtight container for up to 3 days.

GLUTEN-FREE

Replace the cake flour with a scant 1¼ cups (191 g) gluten-free flour blend.

HIGH ALTITUDE

Bake at 350°F for 20 to 25 minutes, until a toothpick inserted in the center comes out clean.

APPLE SPICE MUFFINS

MAKES 12 MUFFINS

When September comes around, all I crave is cinnamon and spice. These muffins use my favorite spice trio—cinnamon, ginger, and cloves. The result is a warm and cozy muffin. Applesauce is a great egg replacer, as it provides moisture and structure, especially in an apple-flavored bake! I usually use Fuji apples for these muffins because I like their sweetness. But you can also use Gala, Cripps Pink, or Pink Lady for a similar flavor.

BATTER

½ cup (113 g) salted butter, softened

½ cup (113 g) cane sugar

¼ cup (57 g) packed dark brown sugar

1 cup (226 g) applesauce, room temperature

2 cups (255 g) all-purpose flour

1 teaspoon baking powder

½ teaspoon fine sea salt

½ teaspoon cinnamon

½ teaspoon cloves

½ teaspoon ginger

1 large Fuji apple, cut into chunks

TOPPING

1 cup (127 g) all-purpose flour

½ cup (113 g) salted butter, melted

½ cup (113 g) cane sugar

2 tablespoons (28 g) packed dark brown sugar

¼ teaspoon cinnamon

GLAZE

½ cup (71 g) powdered sugar, sifted

1½ tablespoons milk

Preheat the oven to 350°F. Line a muffin pan with liners.

TO MAKE THE BATTER: In the bowl of a stand mixer fitted with the paddle attachment, add the butter, cane sugar, and brown sugar. Mix on low until combined and there are no chunks of butter.

Add the applesauce and mix to combine.

Add the flour, baking powder, sea salt, cinnamon, cloves, and ginger in that order and mix on low to combine into a smooth batter. Add the apple chunks and fold with a spatula to combine completely. Fill the muffin liners full with batter.

TO MAKE THE TOPPING: In a medium bowl, add the flour, melted butter, cane sugar, brown sugar, and cinnamon. Stir with a spatula until combined. Crumble the topping on top of the muffin batter.

Bake for 25 to 30 minutes, until a toothpick inserted in the center comes out clean. Allow to cool completely.

TO MAKE THE GLAZE: In a medium bowl, add the powdered sugar and milk and whisk together until you have a smooth glaze. Drizzle over the tops of the muffins.

Store in an airtight container for up to 3 days.

GLUTEN-FREE

Replace the all-purpose flour with 1⅔ cups (255 g) gluten-free flour blend for the batter, and replace the all-purpose flour with ¾ cup plus 1 tablespoon (127 g) gluten-free flour blend for the topping.

HIGH ALTITUDE

Bake at 350°F for 20 to 25 minutes, until a toothpick inserted in the center comes out clean.

MIXED BERRY MUFFINS

MAKES 12 MUFFINS

Fresh berries baked into muffins are an ultimate treat. If you don't have
fresh berries on hand, you can use frozen berries; just be sure to thaw and
strain them in the fridge overnight before using. A trick when making these
is to use tulip baking liners so all the amazing topping stays inside the liners
and doesn't spill over the edges like it may with traditional muffin liners.

BATTER

½ cup (113 g) salted butter,
   softened

½ cup (113 g) cane sugar

¼ cup (57 g) packed light
   brown sugar

1 tablespoon (21 g) raw honey

1 teaspoon vanilla extract

¾ cup (177 ml) milk, room
   temperature

2 large ripe bananas

2 cups (255 g) all-purpose
   flour

1 teaspoon baking powder

½ teaspoon fine sea salt

2 ounces (57 g) blueberries

2 ounces (57 g) blackberries

2 ounces (57 g) raspberries

TOPPING

1 cup (127 g) all-purpose flour

½ cup (113 g) packed light
   brown sugar

¼ cup (25 g) rolled oats

½ cup (113 g) salted butter,
   melted

Preheat the oven to 350°F. Line a muffin tin with liners.

TO MAKE THE BATTER: In the bowl of a stand mixer fitted with the
paddle attachment, add the butter, cane sugar, brown sugar, honey,
and vanilla extract. Mix on low until combined and there are no
chunks of butter.

Add the milk and bananas and mix on low until combined, scraping
down the sides of the bowl as needed.

Add the flour, baking powder, and sea salt in that order and mix on
low to combine into a smooth batter. Add the blueberries, blackberries, and raspberries and fold with a spatula to combine completely. Fill the muffin liners full with batter.

TO MAKE THE TOPPING: In a medium bowl, add the flour, brown
sugar, and oats and swirl together. Add the melted butter and stir
with a spatula until combined. Crumble the topping on top of the
muffin batter.

Bake for 25 to 30 minutes, until a toothpick inserted in the center
comes out clean.

Store in an airtight container for up to 3 days.

GLUTEN-FREE

Use gluten-free oats, replace the
all-purpose flour with 1⅔ cups
(255 g) gluten-free flour blend
for the batter, and replace the
all-purpose flour with ¾ cup
plus 1 tablespoon (127 g) gluten-
free flour blend for the topping.

HIGH ALTITUDE

Bake at 350°F for 20 to
25 minutes, until a toothpick
inserted in the center comes
out clean.

BAKED FRENCH TOAST

MAKES 6 SLICES

This is an amazing recipe to make for a crowd, as you can easily double it or triple it to get more French toast. Cornstarch is what helps this French toast crisp up. It is a natural binder, just like eggs. If you don't want to wait for the slices to bake, you can fry them up in a pan the traditional way too. Just be sure to grease the pan generously with butter. Either way you choose to cook it, this French toast is easy to make and serve for Sunday brunch!

TOAST

1 teaspoon aquafaba powder

¼ cup plus 2 tablespoons (89 ml) water

½ cup (113 g) salted butter, melted

½ cup (118 ml) milk

¼ cup (59 ml) heavy whipping cream

2 teaspoons cinnamon

½ teaspoon cornstarch

¼ teaspoon nutmeg

Six 1-inch slices French bread

FOR SERVING

Powdered sugar

Maple syrup

Bananas

Blueberries

Preheat the oven to 350°F. Line a baking sheet with parchment paper.

In a large bowl, add the aquafaba and water and stir together.

Add the melted butter, milk, whipping cream, cinnamon, cornstarch, and nutmeg and whisk together.

Soak each piece of bread in the mixture and place on the prepared baking sheet.

Bake for 25 to 30 minutes, flipping halfway through.

Dust with powdered sugar, and serve with maple syrup, bananas, and blueberries.

GLUTEN-FREE

Use gluten-free bread.

HIGH ALTITUDE

Bake at 350°F for 22 to 27 minutes, flipping halfway through.

LEMON ROSEMARY SCONES

MAKES 6 SCONES

Lemon and rosemary is one of my favorite sweet and savory combinations. I love the sweet flavor of lemon with the earthy and intense flavor of rosemary. I use yogurt in sweet scones to replace the eggs. Give this substitution a try: You will never have a dry scone with it! These scones make the perfect eggless addition to a Sunday brunch or a Christmas morning breakfast.

DOUGH

2⅓ cups (298 g) all-purpose flour

⅓ cup (75 g) cane sugar

1 tablespoon baking powder

1 teaspoon dried rosemary

½ teaspoon fine sea salt

½ cup (113 g) salted butter, cold

¾ cup (177 ml) heavy whipping cream

¼ cup (57 g) vanilla yogurt

2 teaspoons lemon flavor

Zest of 1 lemon

TOPPING

2 tablespoons (30 ml) heavy whipping cream

1 tablespoon cane sugar

GLUTEN-FREE

Replace the all-purpose flour with 2 cups (310 g) gluten-free flour blend.

HIGH ALTITUDE

Bake at 400°F for 18 to 22 minutes, until lightly golden brown on the bottoms.

Line a baking sheet with parchment paper.

TO MAKE THE DOUGH: In the bowl of a stand mixer fitted with the paddle attachment, add the flour, cane sugar, baking powder, rosemary, and sea salt. Mix on low for two to three rotations to combine the dry ingredients.

Using a large grater, grate the butter and add to the flour mixture. Don't mix yet.

Add the whipping cream, yogurt, lemon flavor, and zest and mix on low to combine. You'll have to scrape the bowl to help combine the dry ingredients, and I find it's easier to finish combining with your hands.

Using your hands, form the dough into a round disk that is about 7 inches in diameter. Using a sharp knife, cut into six triangular pieces like a pie. Separate the pieces so they are spaced evenly apart.

TO MAKE THE TOPPING: In a small dish, add the whipping cream. Using a pastry brush, brush the tops of the scones to coat completely. Sprinkle with the tablespoon of cane sugar.

Place the baking sheet in the fridge for 30 minutes. Preheat the oven to 400°F.

Bake for 20 to 24 minutes, until lightly golden brown on the bottoms. Allow to cool completely on the baking sheet.

Store in a cool dry place for up to 3 days.

HAM, CHEESE & CHIVES SCONES

MAKES 6 SCONES

Sometimes I want an indulgent breakfast, and I want it to fill me up. That's when I make these Ham, Cheese & Chives Scones. Not only are they a treat, but they have added protein with the ham and cheese, so you won't miss that classic omelet! Top these with a pad of butter and breakfast is served.

DOUGH

2⅓ cups (298 g) all-purpose flour

¼ cup (57 g) cane sugar

1 tablespoon baking powder

½ teaspoon fine sea salt

½ teaspoon dried thyme

¼ teaspoon dried sage

½ cup (113 g) salted butter, cold

¾ cup (177 ml) heavy whipping cream

¼ cup (57 g) sour cream

½ cup (45 g) grated cheddar cheese

4 ounces (113 g) honey ham, diced

2 chives, chopped

TOPPING

2 tablespoons (30 ml) heavy whipping cream

GLUTEN-FREE

Replace the all-purpose flour with 2 cups (310 g) gluten-free flour blend.

HIGH ALTITUDE

Bake at 400°F for 18 to 22 minutes, until lightly golden brown on the bottoms.

Line a baking sheet with parchment paper.

TO MAKE THE DOUGH: In the bowl of a stand mixer fitted with the paddle attachment, add the flour, cane sugar, baking powder, sea salt, thyme, and sage. Mix on low for two to three rotations to combine the dry ingredients.

Using a large grater, grate the butter and add to the flour mixture. Don't mix yet.

Add the whipping cream, sour cream, cheese, ham, and chives and mix on low to combine. You'll have to scrape the bowl to help combine the dry ingredients, and I find it's easier to finish combining with your hands.

Using your hands, form the dough into a round disk that is about 7 inches in diameter and place it on the prepared baking sheet. Using a sharp knife, cut into six triangular pieces like a pie. Separate the pieces so they are spaced evenly apart.

TO MAKE THE TOPPING: In a small dish, add the whipping cream. Using a pastry brush, brush the tops of the scones with the cream to coat completely.

Place the baking sheet in the fridge for 30 minutes. Preheat the oven to 400°F.

Bake for 20 to 24 minutes, until lightly golden brown on the bottoms.

Store in the fridge for up to 3 days. Reheat by warming in the oven.

LONDON FOG SCONES

MAKES 6 SCONES

Earl Grey tea is one of my favorites. Its comforting flavor pairs so well with vanilla and milk, hence why London Fog drinks are so popular. These scones are a wonderful addition to your Sunday brunch menu!

DOUGH

2⅓ cups (298 g) all-purpose flour

⅓ cup (75 g) cane sugar

1 tablespoon baking powder

1 bag Earl Grey tea leaves

½ teaspoon fine sea salt

½ cup (113 g) salted butter, cold

¾ cup (177 ml) heavy whipping cream

¼ cup (57 g) vanilla yogurt

1 teaspoon vanilla extract

TOPPING

2 tablespoons (30 ml) heavy whipping cream

GLAZE

1 cup (142 g) powdered sugar, sifted

2 tablespoons (30 ml) milk

GLUTEN-FREE

Replace the all-purpose flour with 2 cups (310 g) gluten-free flour blend.

HIGH ALTITUDE

Bake at 400°F for 18 to 22 minutes, until lightly golden brown on the bottoms.

Line a baking sheet with parchment paper.

TO MAKE THE DOUGH: In the bowl of a stand mixer fitted with the paddle attachment, add the flour, cane sugar, baking powder, Earl Grey tea leaves, and sea salt. Mix on low for two to three rotations to combine the dry ingredients.

Using a large grater, grate the butter and add to the flour mixture. Don't mix yet.

Add the whipping cream, yogurt, and vanilla extract and mix on low to combine. You'll have to scrape the bowl to help combine the dry ingredients, and I find it's easier to finish combining with your hands.

Using your hands, form the dough into a round disk that is about 7 inches in diameter and place it on the prepared baking sheet. Using a sharp knife, cut into six triangular pieces like a pie. Separate the pieces so they are spaced evenly apart.

TO MAKE THE TOPPING: In a small dish, add the whipping cream. Using a pastry brush, brush the tops of the scones with the cream to coat completely.

Place the baking sheet in the fridge for 30 minutes. Preheat the oven to 400°F.

Bake for 20 to 24 minutes, until lightly golden brown on the bottoms. Allow to cool completely on the baking sheet.

TO MAKE THE GLAZE: In a medium bowl, add the powdered sugar and milk and whisk together until you have a smooth glaze. Using a knife or spatula, slather the glaze on top of each scone.

Store in a cool dry place for up to 3 days.

CHEDDAR JALAPEÑO SCONES

MAKES 6 SCONES

I love these scones because you can make them taste a little different depending on what kind of cheddar cheese you use. The recipe calls for jalapeño cheddar cheese, but if you have only sharp cheddar or white cheddar, then you can use those as well! Serve these scones with breakfast sausage for a hearty meal.

DOUGH

2 to 3 jalapeños

2⅓ cups (298 g) all-purpose flour

¼ cup (57 g) cane sugar

1 tablespoon baking powder

½ teaspoon fine sea salt

¼ teaspoon black pepper

½ cup (113 g) salted butter, cold

¾ cup (177 ml) heavy whipping cream

¼ cup (57 g) sour cream

½ cup (45 g) grated jalapeño cheddar cheese

TOPPING

2 tablespoons (30 ml) heavy whipping cream

GLUTEN-FREE

Replace the all-purpose flour with 2 cups (310 g) gluten-free flour blend.

HIGH ALTITUDE

Bake at 400°F for 18 to 22 minutes, until lightly golden brown on the bottoms.

Line a baking sheet with parchment paper.

De-stem the jalapeños, remove the seeds, and dice. Set aside.

TO MAKE THE DOUGH: In the bowl of a stand mixer fitted with the paddle attachment, add the flour, cane sugar, baking powder, sea salt, and black pepper. Mix on low for two to three rotations to combine the dry ingredients.

Using a large grater, grate the butter and add to the flour mixture. Don't mix yet.

Add the whipping cream, sour cream, cheese, and jalapeños and mix on low to combine. You'll have to scrape the bowl to help combine the dry ingredients, and I find it's easier to finish combining with your hands.

Using your hands, form the dough into a round disk that is about 7 inches in diameter and place it on the prepared baking sheet. Using a sharp knife, cut into six triangular pieces like a pie. Separate the pieces so they are spaced evenly apart.

TO MAKE THE TOPPING: In a small dish, add the whipping cream. Using a pastry brush, brush the tops of the scones with the cream to coat completely.

Place the baking sheet in the fridge for 30 minutes. Preheat the oven to 400°F.

Bake for 20 to 24 minutes, until lightly golden brown on the bottoms.

Store in the fridge for up to 3 days. Reheat by warming in the oven.

RASPBERRY GREEN TEA SCONES

MAKES 6 SCONES

Fresh raspberries are used to make the glaze for these scones, and also naturally color it pastel pink. If you have raspberries that are going a little soft, this recipe is the perfect way to use them, as you muddle the raspberries for the glaze! You can use caffeinated or decaf green tea in this recipe, whichever you prefer, as the flavor will still come through.

DOUGH

2⅓ cups (298 g) all-purpose flour

⅓ cup (75 g) cane sugar

1 tablespoon baking powder

1 bag green tea leaves

½ teaspoon fine sea salt

½ cup (113 g) salted butter, cold

¾ cup (177 ml) heavy whipping cream

¼ cup (57 g) vanilla yogurt

1 teaspoon vanilla extract

TOPPING

2 tablespoons (30 ml) heavy whipping cream

GLAZE

3 ounces (85 g) raspberries

2 cups (284 g) powdered sugar, sifted

GLUTEN-FREE

Replace the all-purpose flour with 2 cups (310 g) gluten-free flour blend.

HIGH ALTITUDE

Bake at 400°F for 18 to 22 minutes, until lightly golden brown on the bottoms.

Line a baking sheet with parchment paper.

TO MAKE THE DOUGH: In the bowl of a stand mixer fitted with the paddle attachment, add the flour, cane sugar, baking powder, green tea leaves, and sea salt. Mix on low for two to three rotations to combine the dry ingredients.

Using a large grater, grate the butter and add to the flour mixture. Don't mix yet.

Add the whipping cream, yogurt, and vanilla extract and mix on low to combine. You'll have to scrape the bowl to help combine the dry ingredients, and I find it's easier to finish combining with your hands.

Using your hands, form the dough into a round disk that is about 7 inches in diameter and place it on the prepared baking sheet. Using a sharp knife, cut into six triangular pieces like a pie. Separate the pieces so they are spaced evenly apart.

TO MAKE THE TOPPING: In a small dish, add the whipping cream. Using a pastry brush, brush the tops of the scones with the cream to coat completely.

Place the baking sheet in the fridge for 30 minutes. Preheat the oven to 400°F.

Bake for 20 to 24 minutes, until lightly golden brown on the bottoms. Allow to cool completely on the baking sheet.

TO MAKE THE GLAZE: In a medium bowl, add the raspberries. Muddle them either with a muddler or a wooden spoon. Add the powdered sugar and whisk together until you have a smooth glaze. Using a knife or spatula, slather the glaze on top of each scone.

Store in a cool dry place for up to 3 days.

MAPLE BACON SCONES

MAKES 6 SCONES

Sweet and salty combinations are always what I gravitate toward. And these scones hit all the right notes—a brown sugar scone with a sweet maple glaze, topped with salty bacon. I like to use applewood smoked bacon for a very rustic and hearty flavor.

DOUGH

2⅓ cups (298 g) all-purpose flour

⅓ cup (75 g) packed dark brown sugar

1 tablespoon baking powder

½ teaspoon fine sea salt

¼ teaspoon cinnamon

½ cup (113 g) salted butter, cold

¾ cup (177 ml) heavy whipping cream

¼ cup (57 g) vanilla yogurt

TOPPING

2 tablespoons (30 ml) heavy whipping cream

GLAZE

1 cup (142 g) powdered sugar, sifted

¼ cup (88 g) maple syrup

BACON TOPPING

4 slices bacon, cooked to your liking, chopped

TO MAKE THE DOUGH: In the bowl of a stand mixer fitted with the paddle attachment, add the flour, brown sugar, baking powder, sea salt, and cinnamon. Mix on low for two to three rotations to combine the dry ingredients.

Using a large grater, grate the butter and add to the flour mixture. Don't mix yet.

Add the whipping cream and yogurt and mix on low to combine. You'll have to scrape the bowl to help combine the dry ingredients, and I find it's easier to finish combining with your hands.

Using your hands, form the dough into a round disk that is about 7 inches in diameter and place it on the prepared baking sheet. Using a sharp knife, cut into six triangular pieces like a pie. Separate the pieces so they are spaced evenly apart.

TO MAKE THE TOPPING: In a small dish, add the whipping cream. Using a pastry brush, brush the tops of the scones with the cream to coat completely.

Place the baking sheet in the fridge for 30 minutes. Preheat the oven to 400°F.

Bake for 20 to 24 minutes, until lightly golden brown on the bottoms. Allow to cool completely on the baking sheet.

TO MAKE THE GLAZE: In a medium bowl, add the powdered sugar and maple syrup and whisk together until you have a smooth glaze. Using a knife or spatula, slather the glaze on top of each scone. Top with pieces of bacon.

Store in a cool dry place for up to 3 days.

GLUTEN-FREE

Replace the all-purpose flour with 2 cups (310 g) gluten-free flour blend.

HIGH ALTITUDE

Bake at 400°F for 18 to 22 minutes, until lightly golden brown on the bottoms.

STRAWBERRY TOASTER PASTRIES

MAKES 5 TOASTER PASTRIES

There is a big difference between Pop-Tarts and homemade toaster pastries. And I feel like you're on either one team or another. Personally, I love and appreciate both versions for their differences. These toaster pastries are exactly as I remember them from growing up. The crust is flaky, the filling is fruity. This recipe adds more glaze on top where traditionally there would be egg wash . . . because more glaze is always better!

DOUGH

2 cups (255 g) all-purpose flour

½ teaspoon cane sugar

¾ cup (170 g) salted butter, cold

½ cup (118 ml) cold water

FILLING

6 ounces (170 g) strawberry jam

2 tablespoons (30 ml) water

GLAZE

1 cup (142 g) powdered sugar, sifted

2 tablespoons (30 ml) water

Rainbow sprinkles (optional)

HIGH ALTITUDE

Bake at 350°F for 45 to 50 minutes, until golden brown.

TO MAKE THE DOUGH: In the bowl of a stand mixer fitted with the paddle attachment, add the flour and cane sugar. Turn on low for two to three rotations to combine the dry ingredients.

Remove the butter from the fridge and cut the stick into four pieces and then chop into small cubes from there. The smaller the cubes, the flakier the crust. Add the cold cubed butter to the flour mixture. Measure out the cold water and have it ready.

Turn the mixer on low and slowly start to incorporate the ingredients. Gradually turn the mixer to medium speed. Once the butter mixture looks like wet sand, immediately add in all the cold water. As soon as the dough comes together, stop the mixer.

Form the dough into a rectangle and wrap in plastic wrap. Allow to cool in the fridge for at least 6 hours or overnight before rolling out the dough.

Line a baking sheet with parchment paper.

Remove the plastic wrap from the dough and place on a floured surface. Roll out the dough to a rectangle that is about 20 by 12 inches. Cut into 10 rectangles that are about 4 by 6 inches. Transfer five of them to the prepared baking sheet.

TO MAKE THE FILLING: Add about 1½ tablespoons strawberry jam onto the middle of each rectangle on the parchment paper, leaving a small border. Using your hand, dip your finger into the water and go around the border of one of the rectangles. Then immediately place one of the additional dough rectangles on top, using the water to seal it together. Repeat with the rest of the pastries so each one is topped.

Place the baking sheet in the fridge for 15 to 20 minutes, until the dough is firm. Preheat the oven to 350°F.

Remove the baking sheet from the fridge and, using a fork, crimp the edges around each pastry. Make three vent holes in the middle of each pastry.

Bake for 50 to 55 minutes, until golden brown. Let cool completely on the baking sheets.

TO MAKE THE GLAZE: In a medium bowl, add the powdered sugar and water and whisk together until you have a smooth glaze. Using a spatula or butter knife, spread the glaze onto the tops of each pastry. Top with rainbow sprinkles, if using.

Store in a cool dry place for up to 3 days.

CHOCOLATE TOASTER PASTRIES

MAKES 5 TOASTER PASTRIES

There's nothing better than chocolate for breakfast! I totally feel like a kid again when I eat these in lieu of my usual healthy breakfast. And sometimes, that's just what I need. I prefer to enjoy these with a cold glass of milk.

DOUGH

1⅔ cups (212 g) all-purpose flour

3 tablespoons (15 g) Dutch cocoa powder, sifted

½ teaspoon cane sugar

¾ cup (170 g) salted butter, cold

⅓ cup plus 2 tablespoons (108 ml) cold water

FILLING

2 ounces (57 g) milk chocolate, chopped

2 ounces (57 g) dark chocolate, chopped

¼ cup (59 ml) heavy whipping cream

2 tablespoons (30 ml) water

GLAZE

1 cup (142 g) powdered sugar, sifted

3 tablespoons (15 g) Dutch cocoa powder, sifted

2½ tablespoons (37 ml) water

TOPPING

2 ounces (57 g) dark chocolate, melted

HIGH ALTITUDE

Bake at 350°F for 45 to 50 minutes, until the dough looks dry.

TO MAKE THE DOUGH: In the bowl of a stand mixer fitted with the paddle attachment, add the flour, cocoa, and cane sugar. Turn on low for two to three rotations to combine the dry ingredients.

Remove the butter from the fridge and cut the stick into four pieces and then chop into small cubes from there. The smaller the cubes, the flakier the crust. Add the cold cubed butter to the flour mixture. Measure out the cold water and have it ready.

Turn the mixer on low and slowly start to incorporate the ingredients. Gradually turn the mixer to medium speed. Once the butter mixture looks like wet sand, immediately add in all the cold water. As soon as the dough comes together, stop the mixer.

Form the dough into a rectangle and wrap in plastic wrap. Allow to cool in the fridge for at least 6 hours or overnight before rolling out the dough.

TO MAKE THE FILLING: Using a double boiler, add the milk chocolate and dark chocolate and melt completely. Slowly add the cream and whisk until it is completely combined. Remove from heat and allow to set for at least 4 hours, until firm.

Line a baking sheet with parchment paper.

Remove the plastic wrap from the dough and place on a floured surface. Roll out the dough to a rectangle that is about 20 by 12 inches. Cut into 10 rectangles that are about 4 by 6 inches. Transfer five of them to the prepared baking sheet.

Add about 1½ tablespoons chocolate filling onto the middle of each rectangle on the parchment paper, leaving a small border. Using your hand, dip your finger into the water and go around the border of one of the rectangles. Then immediately place one of the additional dough rectangles onto the middle of a rectangle on the parchment paper, using the water to seal it together. Repeat with the rest of the pastries so each one is topped.

Place the baking sheet in the fridge for 15 to 20 minutes, until the dough is firm. Preheat the oven to 350°F.

Remove the baking sheet from the fridge and, using a fork, crimp the edges around each pastry. Make three vent holes in the middle of each pastry.

Bake for 50 to 55 minutes, until the dough looks dry. Let cool completely on the baking sheet.

TO MAKE THE GLAZE: In a medium bowl, add the powdered sugar, cocoa, and water and whisk together until you have a smooth glaze. Using a spatula or butter knife, spread the glaze onto the tops of each pastry.

Drizzle the tops with the melted dark chocolate.

Store in a cool dry place for up to 3 days.

BLUEBERRY GINGER COFFEE CAKE

MAKES A 9-INCH CAKE

Coffee cake was always reserved for special occasions when I was growing up, so I've always associated it with celebrations or holidays. It's partially why I love making coffee cake now, as I can make a normal day feel like a celebration. I use a combination of yogurt and sour cream to create a luscious coffee cake. It has an identical texture to traditional coffee cake made with eggs, but it's even moister! This is probably one of my favorite recipes in the entire book.

BATTER

½ cup (113 g) salted butter, softened

¾ cup (170 g) cane sugar

½ cup (118 ml) milk, room temperature

½ cup (113 g) vanilla yogurt, room temperature

¼ cup (57 g) sour cream, room temperature

1⅔ cups (212 g) all-purpose flour

2½ tablespoons (14 g) coconut flour

1 teaspoon baking powder

½ teaspoon ginger

½ teaspoon fine sea salt

6 ounces (170 g) blueberries

TOPPING

¾ cup (95 g) all-purpose flour

½ cup (113 g) cane sugar

½ teaspoon cinnamon

½ teaspoon ginger

6 tablespoons (85 g) salted butter, melted

GLAZE

1 cup (142 g) powdered sugar, sifted

2 tablespoons (30 ml) water

Preheat the oven to 375°F. Line a 9-inch cake pan with parchment paper.

TO MAKE THE BATTER: In the bowl of a stand mixer fitted with the paddle attachment, add the butter and cane sugar. Mix on low until combined and no chunks of butter remain. Add the milk, yogurt, and sour cream and mix on low until combined.

In a separate bowl, add the flour, coconut flour, baking powder, ginger, and sea salt and whisk together. With the mixer on low, slowly add the flour mixture to the butter mixture and continue to mix on low until combined into a smooth batter, scraping down the sides of the bowl as needed. Fold in the blueberries.

Transfer the batter into the prepared cake pan and spread out evenly. Bake for 20 minutes. Set a timer. While the cake is baking, prepare the topping.

TO MAKE THE TOPPING: Add the flour, cane sugar, cinnamon, and ginger to a medium bowl and swirl together. Add the melted butter and fold together with a spatula until you have a paste.

Once the timer goes off, remove the cake from the oven and, using your hands, crumble the topping onto the partially baked cake batter. Return the cake to the oven and bake for 20 minutes, or until a toothpick inserted in the center comes out clean. Allow the cake to cool completely before removing from the pan.

TO MAKE THE GLAZE: In a medium bowl, add the powdered sugar and water and whisk together until you have a smooth glaze. Using a pastry brush, brush the glaze on top of the cake.

Store in an airtight container for up to 3 days.

GLUTEN-FREE

Replace the all-purpose flour in the batter with 1⅓ cups (212 g) gluten-free flour blend, and replace the all-purpose flour in the topping with ½ cup plus 1 tablespoon (95 g) gluten-free flour blend.

HIGH ALTITUDE

Bake at 375°F for 15 minutes. After the topping is added, bake for 20 minutes, or until a toothpick inserted in the center comes out clean.

⊘
GLUTEN-FREE

Replace the all-purpose flour in
the batter with 1⅓ cups (212 g)
gluten-free flour blend, and
replace the all-purpose flour
in the topping with ½ cup plus
1 tablespoon (95 g) gluten-free
flour blend.

▲▲
HIGH ALTITUDE

Bake at 375°F for 15 minutes.
After the topping is added,
bake for 20 minutes, or until a
toothpick inserted in the center
comes out clean.

CINNAMON SWIRL COFFEE CAKE

MAKES A 9-INCH CAKE

Coffee cake has always reminded me of Christmas, as my mom always made sure we had one from a local bakery during that time. One bite still takes me back to that magical time of year. I am carrying on that tradition in my house every year when I make coffee cake during Christmas.

BATTER

½ cup (113 g) salted butter, softened

¾ cup (170 g) cane sugar

1 teaspoon vanilla extract

½ cup (118 ml) milk, room temperature

½ cup (113 g) vanilla yogurt, room temperature

¼ cup (57 g) sour cream, room temperature

1⅔ cups (212 g) all-purpose flour

2½ tablespoons (14 g) coconut flour

1 teaspoon baking powder

½ teaspoon cinnamon

½ teaspoon fine sea salt

CINNAMON SWIRL

¼ cup (57 g) packed dark brown sugar

1 tablespoon milk

1 teaspoon cinnamon

TOPPING

¾ cup (95 g) all-purpose flour

½ cup (113 g) cane sugar

½ teaspoon cinnamon

6 tablespoons (85 g) salted butter, melted

GLAZE

1 cup (142 g) powdered sugar, sifted

2 tablespoons (30 ml) water

Preheat the oven to 375°F. Line a 9-inch cake pan with parchment paper.

TO MAKE THE BATTER: In the bowl of a stand mixer fitted with the paddle attachment, add the butter, cane sugar, and vanilla extract. Mix on low until combined and no chunks of butter remain. Add the milk, yogurt, and sour cream and mix on low until combined.

In a separate bowl, add the flour, coconut flour, baking powder, cinnamon, and sea salt and whisk together. With the mixer on low, slowly add the flour mixture to the butter mixture and continue to mix on low until combined into a smooth batter, scraping down the sides of the bowl as needed.

TO MAKE THE CINNAMON SWIRL: In a small bowl, add the brown sugar, milk, and cinnamon and mix to combine completely.

Transfer half the batter into the prepared cake pan and spread out evenly. Then add the cinnamon swirl mixture by drizzling it on top of the batter in a spiral. Then add the remaining batter on top, spreading evenly.

Bake for 20 minutes. Set a timer. While the cake is baking, get the topping ready.

TO MAKE THE TOPPING: Add the flour, cane sugar, and cinnamon, to a medium bowl and swirl together. Add the melted butter and fold together with a spatula until you have a paste.

Once the timer goes off, remove the cake from the oven and, using your hands, crumble the topping onto the partially baked cake batter. Return the cake to the oven and bake for 20 minutes, or until a toothpick inserted in the center comes out clean. Allow the cake to cool completely before removing from the pan.

TO MAKE THE GLAZE: In a medium bowl, add the powdered sugar and water and whisk together until you have a smooth glaze. Using a pastry brush, brush the glaze on top of the cake.

Store in an airtight container for up to 3 days.

CINNAMON ROLLS

MAKES 8 CINNAMON ROLLS

Cinnamon rolls are a classic Saturday morning treat. Traditionally, egg is one of the main ingredients in brioche dough, which is used for cinnamon rolls. And there are usually two rises. However, these cinnamon rolls require only one rise. What's more, they are so fluffy and perfectly moist you wouldn't ever know they were any different from the traditional version. I even prefer these to my traditional cinnamon rolls!

DOUGH

1 tablespoon (10 g) active dry yeast

¼ cup (57 g) plus ½ teaspoon cane sugar

¼ cup (59 ml) warm water

¼ cup (57 g) salted butter

1 cup (237 ml) milk

1 teaspoon raw honey

3½ cups (446 g) all-purpose flour

1 teaspoon fine sea salt

FILLING

¾ cup (170 g) packed dark brown sugar

2 tablespoons cinnamon

¼ cup (57 g) salted butter, softened

GLAZE

Heaping 2⅓ cups (340 g) powdered sugar, sifted

¼ cup milk

HIGH ALTITUDE

Bake at 350°F for 35 minutes, or until golden brown.

TO MAKE THE DOUGH: In the bowl of a stand mixer fitted with the dough hook, add the yeast, ½ teaspoon cane sugar, and warm water. Stir to combine and let sit for 5 minutes, until bubbly.

In a small pot over medium heat, add the butter, milk, and honey. Stir until completely melted; remove from heat.

Add the flour, remaining ¼ cup cane sugar, and sea salt to the mixing bowl in that order. Add the milk mixture and knead on speed 2 to 4 for 5 minutes.

Place the dough in a greased bowl, then cover the bowl with a kitchen towel and let rise for 2 to 3 hours, until doubled in size.

Preheat the oven to 350°F and grease a baking dish, either a 9-inch round dish or an 11-by-7-inch dish.

TO MAKE THE FILLING: In a small bowl, add the brown sugar and cinnamon and mix to combine completely.

On a floured surface, roll out the dough to a rectangle that is about 12 by 16 inches. Using a spatula, spread the butter all over the rolled-out dough.

Sprinkle the brown sugar and cinnamon mixture to completely cover the butter.

Starting at the longer side, fold the dough over and start to roll the dough until it is completely rolled into a log. Trim off each of the ends, then cut the dough log into eight cinnamon rolls. Place in the greased baking dish.

Bake for 40 minutes, or until golden brown. Let rest for 10 minutes.

TO MAKE THE GLAZE: In a medium bowl, add the powdered sugar and milk and whisk together until you have a smooth glaze. Slather the glaze over the tops of the warm cinnamon rolls.

Store in an airtight container for up to 3 days.

CHOCOLATE PEANUT BUTTER HONEY SWEET ROLLS

MAKES 8 SWEET ROLLS

Chocolate sweet rolls are one of my favorite pastries. Like their cinnamon-filled friends, chocolate sweet rolls are fluffy and covered in glaze, but they aren't as sweet, which is part of what I love about them. I've added peanut butter and honey to these for a sweet and salty pastry that you're sure to love!

DOUGH

1 tablespoon (10 g) active dry yeast

¼ cup (57 g) plus ½ teaspoon cane sugar

¼ cup (59 ml) warm water

¼ cup (57 g) salted butter

1 cup (237 ml) milk

1 teaspoon raw honey

3½ cups (446 g) all-purpose flour

1 teaspoon fine sea salt

FILLING

¼ cup (57 g) salted butter, softened

2 tablespoons (32 g) peanut butter

½ cup (113 g) cane sugar

¼ cup (21 g) Dutch cocoa powder, sifted

GLAZE

Heaping 2⅓ cups (340 g) powdered sugar, sifted

¼ cup (59 ml) milk

1 teaspoon raw honey

HIGH ALTITUDE

Bake at 350°F for 35 minutes, or until golden brown.

TO MAKE THE DOUGH: In the bowl of a stand mixer fitted with the dough hook, add the yeast, ½ teaspoon cane sugar, and warm water. Stir to combine and let sit for 5 minutes, until bubbly.

In a small pot over medium heat, add the butter, milk, and honey. Stir until completely melted; remove from heat.

Add the flour, remaining ¼ cup cane sugar, and sea salt to the mixing bowl in that order. Add the milk mixture and knead on speed 2 to 4 for 5 minutes.

Place the dough in a greased bowl, then cover the bowl with a kitchen towel and let rise for 2 to 3 hours, until doubled in size.

Preheat the oven to 350°F and grease a baking dish, either a 9-inch round dish or an 11-by-7-inch dish.

TO MAKE THE FILLING: In a small bowl, add the butter and peanut butter and beat with a hand mixer or stir vigorously to combine completely. In a separate bowl, add the cane sugar and cocoa and combine completely.

On a floured surface, roll out the dough to a rectangle that is about 12 by 16 inches. Using a spatula, spread the butter mixture all over the rolled-out dough.

Sprinkle the cocoa and sugar mixture to completely cover the butter.

Starting at the longer side, fold the dough over and start to roll the dough until it is completely rolled into a log. Trim off each of the ends, then cut the dough log into eight sweet rolls. Place in a greased baking dish.

Bake for 40 minutes or until golden brown. Let rest for 10 minutes.

TO MAKE THE GLAZE: In a medium bowl, add the powdered sugar, milk, and honey and whisk together until you have a smooth glaze. Slather the glaze over the tops of the warm sweet rolls.

Store in an airtight container for up to 3 days.

CHOCOLATE RASPBERRY SWEET ROLLS

MAKES 8 SWEET ROLLS

I love filling sweet rolls with fresh fruit. However, very sweet and juicy fruits such as raspberries need to be accompanied by flour and cornstarch. Both of these ingredients help thicken the fruit juice so you get a true raspberry flavor and texture inside. Without these thickeners, the filling will evaporate and leak out of the sweet rolls. So, while it may seem odd to add these two ingredients inside a sweet and fluffy pastry, they are completely necessary!

DOUGH

1 tablespoon (10 g) active dry yeast

¼ cup (57 g) plus ½ teaspoon cane sugar

¼ cup (59 ml) warm water

¼ cup (57 g) salted butter

1 cup (237 ml) milk

1 teaspoon raw honey

3½ cups (446 g) all-purpose flour

1 teaspoon fine sea salt

FILLING

6 ounces (170 g) raspberries

¼ cup (57 g) cane sugar

3 tablespoons (21 g) all-purpose flour

1 teaspoon cornstarch

¼ cup (57 g) salted butter, softened

GLAZE

1 cup (142 g) powdered sugar, sifted

3 tablespoons (15 g) Dutch cocoa powder, sifted

2½ tablespoons (37 ml) water

HIGH ALTITUDE

Bake at 350°F for 35 minutes, or until golden brown.

TO MAKE THE DOUGH: In the bowl of a stand mixer fitted with the dough hook, add the yeast, ½ teaspoon cane sugar, and warm water. Stir to combine and let sit for 5 minutes, until bubbly.

In a small pot over medium heat, add the butter, milk, and honey. Stir until completely melted; remove from heat.

Add the flour, remaining ¼ cup cane sugar, and sea salt to the mixing bowl in that order. Add the milk mixture and knead on speed 2 to 4 for 5 minutes.

Place the dough in a greased bowl, then cover the bowl with a kitchen towel and let rise for 2 to 3 hours, until doubled in size.

Preheat the oven to 350°F and grease a baking dish, either a 9-inch round dish or an 11-by-7-inch dish.

TO MAKE THE FILLING: In a medium bowl, add the raspberries, cane sugar, flour, and cornstarch and stir together to combine. Then squish and break the raspberries with a spatula and you have a raspberry paste.

On a floured surface, roll out the dough to a rectangle that is about 12 by 16 inches. Using a spatula, spread the butter all over the dough, then top with the raspberry paste.

Starting at the longer side, fold the dough over and start to roll the dough until it is completely rolled into a log. Trim off each of the ends, then cut the dough log into eight sweet rolls. Place in a greased baking dish.

Bake for 40 minutes or until golden brown. Let rest for 10 minutes.

TO MAKE THE GLAZE: In a medium bowl, add the powdered sugar, cocoa, and water and whisk together until you have a smooth glaze. Slather the glaze over the tops of the warm sweet rolls.

Store in an airtight container for up to 3 days.

LEMON BLUEBERRY CINNAMON ROLLS

MAKES 8 CINNAMON ROLLS

I use cane sugar in these cinnamon rolls as opposed to brown sugar, which I use in my traditional cinnamon rolls. I also go light on the cinnamon, which allows the blueberries and cinnamon to complement each other in a wonderful way. Topped with a sweet and tart lemon glaze, these are cinnamon rolls you'll want to make over and over!

DOUGH

1 tablespoon (10 g) active dry yeast

¼ cup (57 g) plus ½ teaspoon cane sugar

¼ cup (59 ml) warm water

¼ cup (57 g) salted butter

1 cup (237 ml) milk

1 teaspoon raw honey

3½ cups (446 g) all-purpose flour

1 teaspoon fine sea salt

FILLING

½ cup (113 g) cane sugar

2 teaspoons cinnamon

¼ cup (57 g) salted butter, softened

6 ounces (170 g) blueberries

GLAZE

Heaping 2⅓ cups (340 g) powdered sugar, sifted

2 tablespoons (30 ml) milk

2 tablespoons (30 ml) lemon juice

Zest of 1 lemon for topping

HIGH ALTITUDE

Bake at 350°F for 35 minutes, or until golden brown.

TO MAKE THE DOUGH: In the bowl of a stand mixer fitted with the dough hook, add the yeast, ½ teaspoon cane sugar, and warm water. Stir to combine and let sit for 5 minutes, until bubbly.

In a small pot over medium heat, add the butter, milk, and honey. Stir until completely melted; remove from heat.

Add the flour, remaining ¼ cup cane sugar, and sea salt to the mixing bowl in that order. Add the milk mixture and knead on speed 2 to 4 for 5 minutes.

Place the dough in a greased bowl, then cover the bowl with a kitchen towel and let rise for 2 to 3 hours, until doubled in size.

Preheat the oven to 350°F and grease a baking dish, either a 9-inch round dish or an 11-by-7-inch dish.

TO MAKE THE FILLING: In a small bowl, add the cane sugar and cinnamon and mix together.

On a floured surface, roll out the dough to a rectangle that is about 12 by 16 inches. Using a spatula, spread the butter all over the rolled-out dough.

Sprinkle the cinnamon and sugar mixture on top. Add the blueberries on top, lightly pressing them into the dough.

Starting at the longer side, fold the dough over and start to roll the dough until it is completely rolled into a log. Trim off each of the ends, then cut the dough log into eight cinnamon rolls. Place in the greased baking dish.

Bake for 40 minutes, or until golden brown. Let rest for 10 minutes.

TO MAKE THE GLAZE: In a medium bowl, add the powdered sugar, milk, and lemon juice and whisk together until you have a smooth glaze. Slather the glaze over the tops of the warm cinnamon rolls and top with lemon zest.

Store in an airtight container for up to 3 days.

BROWN SUGAR BANANA CINNAMON ROLLS

MAKES 8 CINNAMON ROLLS

These cinnamon rolls use light brown sugar. As a result, they are a little lighter in flavor than traditional cinnamon rolls. What's more, these rolls have a pinch of nutmeg, fresh banana slices, and pecans that combine to make a warm and cozy treat that's perfect for the holidays.

DOUGH

1 tablespoon (10 g) active dry yeast

¼ cup (57 g) plus ½ teaspoon cane sugar

¼ cup (59 ml) warm water

¼ cup (57 g) salted butter

1 cup (237 ml) milk

1 teaspoon raw honey

3½ cups (446 g) all-purpose flour

1 teaspoon fine sea salt

FILLING

¾ cup (170 g) packed light brown sugar

1 tablespoon cinnamon

Pinch of nutmeg

¼ cup (57 g) salted butter, softened

2 large bananas, sliced

1 cup (127 g) pecans, chopped

GLAZE

1 cup (142 g) powdered sugar, sifted

¼ cup (57 g) cream cheese

1 tablespoon milk

HIGH ALTITUDE

Bake at 350°F for 35 minutes, or until golden brown.

TO MAKE THE DOUGH: In the bowl of a stand mixer fitted with the dough hook, add the yeast, ½ teaspoon cane sugar, and warm water. Stir to combine and let sit for 5 minutes, until bubbly.

In a small pot over medium heat, add the butter, milk, and honey. Stir until completely melted; remove from heat.

Add the flour, remaining ¼ cup cane sugar, and sea salt to the mixing bowl in that order. Add the milk mixture and knead on speed 2 to 4 for 5 minutes.

Place the dough in a greased bowl, then cover the bowl with a kitchen towel and let rise for 2 to 3 hours, until doubled in size.

Preheat the oven to 350°F and grease a baking dish, either a 9-inch round dish or an 11-by-7-inch dish.

TO MAKE THE FILLING: In a small bowl, add the brown sugar, cinnamon, and nutmeg and mix to combine completely.

On a floured surface, roll out the dough to a rectangle that is about 12 by 16 inches. Using a spatula, spread the butter all over the rolled-out dough.

Sprinkle the brown sugar and cinnamon mixture to completely cover the butter. Add the banana slices evenly and then sprinkle with the chopped pecans.

Starting at the longer side, fold the dough over and start to roll the dough until it is completely rolled into a log. Trim off each of the ends, then cut the dough log into eight cinnamon rolls. Place in a greased baking dish.

Bake for 40 minutes, or until golden brown. Let rest for 10 minutes.

TO MAKE THE GLAZE: In a medium bowl, add the powdered sugar, cream cheese, and milk and whisk together until you have a smooth glaze. Slather the glaze over the tops of the warm cinnamon rolls.

Store in an airtight container for up to 3 days.

Breads & Loaf Cakes

Of all the cakes, loaf cakes are what I adore the most! Their cute little shape and thick slices invite just the right ratio of glaze or frosting to cake. It's the perfect ratio, in my opinion. I also love how you can glaze or frost them depending on what you prefer. Not only that, but loaf cakes are one of the easiest cakes to bake and they look seriously impressive!

Loaf cakes can be casual, like my Chocolate Walnut Banana Bread (page 72), or they can be drop-dead gorgeous, like my Vanilla Cherry Loaf Cake (page 88). All the recipes in this chapter use the same size pan, a 1-pound loaf pan. This means you need only one pan to bake whatever you're in the mood for. It couldn't be easier.

For the loaf cakes in this chapter, I use common ingredients you probably already have at home to replace the eggs. You may notice that nothing seems out of the ordinary in these loaf cake recipes, and you are absolutely right! By using the right ratios of ingredients, you can mimic the exact texture of moist and fluffy cake using regular ingredients like milk, heavy whipping cream, and sour cream—ingredients that are commonly found in cake with eggs!

My Classic Banana Bread (page 71) also makes the best gift. Here's a tip from my grandma, who used to bake challah bread like it was her job, as she just truly loved it. She would make 1-pound loaves and give them as gifts simply by wrapping the entire loaf in foil and tying a beautiful ribbon around it. I loved seeing those shiny silver loaves under the tree, all with different-colored ribbons waiting to be given to her friends. Christmas and holiday gifting couldn't be easier—Carrot Zucchini Loaf Cake (page 75), Chocolate Pecan Babka (page 91), and Orange Cardamom Loaf Cake (page 84) would all make delicious presents! Just be sure to wrap them in plastic wrap first, and then foil, so your loaf cakes stay fresh and moist.

CLASSIC BANANA BREAD

MAKES A 1-POUND LOAF

Banana bread can be breakfast, brunch, snack, or even dessert. This versatile little bread is good any time of day! Make sure to use overly ripe bananas for the best banana bread.

½ cup (113 g) salted butter, softened

½ cup (113 g) packed dark brown sugar

¼ cup (57 g) cane sugar

1 teaspoon vanilla extract

2 large ripe bananas

¼ cup (59 ml) heavy whipping cream, room temperature

¼ cup (57 g) sour cream, room temperature

2 cups (255 g) all-purpose flour

¾ teaspoon baking powder

½ teaspoon fine sea salt

½ teaspoon cinnamon

¼ teaspoon cloves

Preheat the oven to 350°F. Line a 1-pound loaf pan with parchment paper, letting it fold over the sides for easier removal.

In the bowl of a stand mixer fitted with the paddle attachment, add the butter, brown sugar, cane sugar, and vanilla extract. Mix on low until combined and there are no chunks of butter.

Add the bananas, whipping cream, and sour cream and mix on low until combined. Scrape down the sides of the bowl and mix again.

Add the flour, baking powder, sea salt, cinnamon, and cloves in that order. Mix on low until combined, scraping down the sides of the bowl as needed. Transfer the batter to the prepared pan.

Bake for 1 hour, or until a toothpick inserted in the center comes out clean. Allow to cool in the pan completely.

Store in an airtight container for up to 7 days.

GLUTEN-FREE

Replace the all-purpose flour with 1⅔ cups (255 g) gluten-free flour blend.

HIGH ALTITUDE

Bake at 350°F for 45 minutes, or until a toothpick inserted in the center comes out clean.

CHOCOLATE WALNUT BANANA BREAD

MAKES A 1-POUND LOAF

Banana bread gets a makeover with lots of chocolate and a generous help-ing of walnuts. This banana bread is more than just a snack—it can count as dessert! Make sure to serve it with a tall glass of milk.

BATTER

½ cup (113 g) salted butter, softened

¾ cup (170 g) packed light brown sugar

1 teaspoon vanilla extract

2 large ripe bananas

½ cup (118 ml) heavy whipping cream, room temperature

¼ cup (57 g) sour cream, room temperature

1⅔ cups (212 g) all-purpose flour

½ cup (43 g) Dutch cocoa powder, sifted

¾ teaspoon baking powder

½ teaspoon fine sea salt

½ teaspoon cinnamon

½ teaspoon ground vanilla bean

FROSTING

1 cup (142 g) powdered sugar, sifted

⅓ cup (28 g) Dutch cocoa powder, sifted

¼ cup (57 g) salted butter, softened

2 tablespoons milk

TOPPING

½ cup (57 g) walnuts, chopped

Preheat the oven to 350°F. Line a 1-pound loaf pan with parchment paper, letting it fold over the sides for easier removal.

TO MAKE THE BATTER: In the bowl of a stand mixer fitted with the paddle attachment, add the butter, brown sugar, and vanilla extract. Mix on low until combined and there are no chunks of butter.

Add the bananas, whipping cream, and sour cream and mix on low until combined. Scrape down the sides of the bowl and mix again.

Add the flour, cocoa, baking powder, sea salt, cinnamon, and ground vanilla bean in that order. Mix on low until combined, scraping down the sides of the bowl as needed. Transfer batter to the prepared pan.

Bake for 1 hour, or until a toothpick inserted in the center comes out clean. Allow to cool completely in the pan.

TO MAKE THE FROSTING: In the bowl of a stand mixer fitted with the paddle attachment, add the powdered sugar, cocoa, butter, and milk. Mix on low until combined and then speed up the mixer to high for 1 minute or until light and fluffy.

Spread the frosting over the top of the loaf and sprinkle with chopped walnuts.

Store in an airtight container for up to 7 days.

GLUTEN-FREE

Replace the all-purpose flour with 1⅓ cups (212 g) gluten-free flour blend.

HIGH ALTITUDE

Bake at 350°F for 45 minutes, until a toothpick inserted in the center comes out clean.

CARROT ZUCCHINI LOAF CAKE

MAKES A 1-POUND LOAF CAKE

I love carrot cake and I love zucchini bread—so I've put them together in this cake. Adding vegetables to cakes always makes for a super-moist cake, and they really help here because there are no eggs. I top this one with a tangy cream cheese frosting.

BATTER

3 ounces (85 g) carrots, finely grated

3 ounces (85 g) zucchini, finely grated

½ cup (118 ml) canola oil

½ cup (113 g) cane sugar

½ cup (113 g) packed light brown sugar

½ cup (118 ml) heavy whipping cream

1¾ cups (223 g) all-purpose flour

1 teaspoon baking powder

1 teaspoon cinnamon

½ teaspoon fine sea salt

¼ teaspoon nutmeg

FROSTING

1 cup plus 3 tablespoons (170 g) powdered sugar, sifted

¼ cup (57 g) salted butter, softened

¼ cup (57 g) cream cheese

½ teaspoon vanilla extract

Preheat the oven to 350°F. Line a 1-pound loaf pan with parchment paper, letting it fold over the sides for easier removal.

TO MAKE THE BATTER: In the bowl of a stand mixer fitted with the paddle attachment, add the carrots, zucchini, canola oil, cane sugar, brown sugar, and heavy whipping cream and mix to combine completely.

Add the flour, baking powder, cinnamon, sea salt, and nutmeg in that order and mix to combine completely until a smooth batter forms.

Pour the batter into the prepared baking pan. Bake for 1 hour, or until a toothpick inserted in the center comes out clean. Allow to cool completely in the pan.

TO MAKE THE FROSTING: In the bowl of a stand mixer fitted with the paddle attachment, add the powdered sugar, butter, cream cheese, and vanilla extract. Mix on low until combined and then speed up the mixer to high for 1 minute, or until light and fluffy.

Spread the frosting over the top of the loaf cake.

Store in an airtight container in the fridge for up to 3 days.

GLUTEN-FREE

Replace the all-purpose flour with a scant 1½ cups (223 g) gluten-free flour blend.

HIGH ALTITUDE

Bake at 350°F for 45 minutes, or until a toothpick inserted into the center comes out clean.

PEANUT BUTTER APPLE LOAF CAKE

MAKES A 1-POUND LOAF CAKE

Autumn in a cake! You'll find comforting fall spices like cinnamon, cloves, and cardamom in this moist apple cake. Topped with peanut butter buttercream, the result is a sweet and salty dessert you're sure to love.

BATTER

½ cup (113 g) applesauce

½ cup (118 ml) canola oil

½ cup (113 g) cane sugar

½ cup (113 g) packed dark brown sugar

½ cup (118 ml) milk

1¾ cups (223 g) all-purpose flour

1 teaspoon baking powder

1 teaspoon cinnamon

½ teaspoon fine sea salt

¼ teaspoon cloves

¼ teaspoon cardamom

FROSTING

1 cup (142 g) powdered sugar, sifted

¼ cup (57 g) salted butter, softened

2 tablespoons (32 g) peanut butter

1 to 2 tablespoons milk

Preheat the oven to 350°F. Line a 1-pound loaf pan with parchment paper, letting it fold over the sides for easier removal.

TO MAKE THE BATTER: In the bowl of a stand mixer fitted with the paddle attachment, add the applesauce, canola oil, cane sugar, brown sugar, and milk and mix on low until combined.

Add the flour, baking powder, cinnamon, sea salt, cloves, and cardamom in that order and mix to combine completely until a smooth batter forms.

Pour the batter into the prepared baking pan. Bake for 1 hour, or until a toothpick inserted in the center comes out clean. Allow to cool completely in the pan.

TO MAKE THE FROSTING: In the bowl of a stand mixer fitted with the paddle attachment, add the powdered sugar, butter, peanut butter, and milk. Mix on low until combined and then speed up the mixer to high for 1 minute, or until light and fluffy.

Spread the frosting over the top of the loaf cake.

Store in an airtight container for up to 3 days.

GLUTEN-FREE

Replace the all-purpose flour with a scant 1½ cups (223 g) gluten-free flour blend.

HIGH ALTITUDE

Bake at 350°F for 45 minutes, or until a toothpick inserted into the center comes out clean.

EARL GREY LEMON LOAF CAKE

MAKES A 1-POUND LOAF CAKE

Earl Grey tea is one of the most popular teas, and its unique bold flavor lends well to the sweet and tartness of fresh lemons. Tea time is extra special with this complementary pair!

BATTER

1 cup (237 ml) milk

2 bags Earl Grey tea

½ cup (113 g) salted butter, softened

¾ cup (170 g) cane sugar

1 teaspoon vanilla extract

¼ cup (57 g) sour cream, room temperature

1¾ cups (248 g) cake flour

1 teaspoon baking powder

½ teaspoon fine sea salt

GLAZE

1½ cups (212 g) powdered sugar, sifted

3 tablespoons lemon juice

Zest of 1 lemon for topping

GLUTEN-FREE

Replace the cake flour with a scant 1⅔ cups (248 g) gluten-free flour blend.

HIGH ALTITUDE

Bake at 350°F for 45 minutes, or until a toothpick inserted into the center comes out clean.

Preheat the oven to 350°F. Line a 1-pound loaf pan with parchment paper, letting it fold over the sides for easier removal.

TO MAKE THE BATTER: Add the milk to a small saucepan and heat until it reaches 140°F on a drink thermometer. Remove from heat and add 1 of the Earl Grey tea bags. Steep for 5 minutes, then remove. Set milk aside and allow to come to room temperature.

In the bowl of a stand mixer fitted with the paddle attachment, add the butter, cane sugar, and vanilla extract. Mix on low until combined and there are no butter chunks.

Add the milk and sour cream and mix on low to combine, scraping down the sides of the bowl to mix in any butter that may stick to the sides.

In a separate bowl, add the cake flour, baking powder, sea salt, and the contents of the remaining Earl Grey tea bag. Whisk together to combine. With the mixer on low, slowly add in the cake flour mixture and mix until combined and you have a smooth cake batter, scraping down the sides of the bowl as needed.

Pour the batter into the prepared baking pan. Bake for 1 hour, or until a toothpick inserted in the center comes out clean. Allow to cool completely in the pan.

TO MAKE THE GLAZE: In a medium bowl, add the powdered sugar and lemon juice and whisk until a smooth glaze forms.

Spread the glaze over the top of the loaf cake and top with lemon zest.

Store in an airtight container for up to 3 days.

RASPBERRY-GLAZED LEMON POPPY SEED LOAF CAKE

MAKES A 1-POUND LOAF CAKE

Fresh lemon juice and fresh raspberries make this loaf cake light and tangy. This is the perfect summer dessert for any occasion. I like to pair it with a scoop of vanilla bean ice cream for a simple but impressive dessert.

BATTER

½ cup (113 g) salted butter, softened

¾ cup (170 g) cane sugar

2 teaspoons lemon flavor

¾ cup milk (177 ml), room temperature

¼ cup (59 ml) fresh lemon juice (about half a lemon)

¼ cup (57 g) sour cream, room temperature

1¾ cups (248 g) cake flour

1 tablespoon (10 g) poppy seeds

1 teaspoon baking powder

½ teaspoon fine sea salt

GLAZE

5 ounces (142 g) raspberries

¼ cup (57 g) cane sugar

¼ cup (59 ml) water

1 cup (142 g) powdered sugar, sifted

GLUTEN-FREE

Replace the cake flour with a scant 1⅔ cups (248 g) gluten-free flour blend.

HIGH ALTITUDE

Bake at 350°F for 45 minutes, or until a toothpick inserted in the center comes out clean.

Preheat the oven to 350°F. Line a 1-pound loaf pan with parchment paper, letting it fold over the sides for easier removal.

TO MAKE THE BATTER: In the bowl of a stand mixer fitted with the paddle attachment, add the butter, cane sugar, and lemon flavor. Mix on low until combined and there are no butter chunks.

Add the milk, lemon juice, and sour cream and mix on low to combine, scraping down the sides of the bowl to mix in any butter that may stick to the sides.

In a separate bowl, add the cake flour, poppy seeds, baking powder, and sea salt. Whisk together to combine. With the mixer on low, slowly add in the flour mixture and mix until combined and you have a smooth cake batter, scraping down the sides of the bowl as needed.

Pour the batter into the prepared baking pan. Bake for 1 hour, or until a toothpick inserted in the center comes out clean. Allow to cool completely in the pan.

TO MAKE THE GLAZE: In a small saucepan, add the raspberries, cane sugar, and water. Put over medium heat and stir to combine. The sugar will dissolve into the water and the berries will start to burst. Allow the mixture to cook until it has reduced by about half, 5 to 10 minutes. Remove from the heat. Cool in the fridge or allow to come to room temperature before using.

In a medium bowl, add the raspberry compote and the powdered sugar and whisk together until you have a smooth glaze. Spread the glaze on top of the loaf cake.

Store in an airtight container for up to 3 days.

SPRINKLE DONUT LOAF CAKE

MAKES A 1-POUND LOAF CAKE

My favorite kind of donuts are old-fashioned cake donuts. Their unique and nostalgic flavor gets me every single time! But I'll let you in on a secret: The right amount of nutmeg in the batter and a perfect glaze is what really what makes them so special. And this cake has both!

BATTER

½ cup (113 g) salted butter, softened

¾ cup (170 g) cane sugar

1 teaspoon vanilla extract

1 cup (237 ml) milk, room temperature

¼ cup (57 g) sour cream, room temperature

1¾ cups (248 g) cake flour

1 teaspoon baking powder

½ teaspoon fine sea salt

¼ teaspoon nutmeg

GLAZE

1 cup (142 g) powdered sugar, sifted

2 tablespoons milk

Rainbow sprinkles for topping

Preheat the oven to 350°F. Line a 1-pound loaf pan with parchment paper, letting it fold over the sides for easier removal.

TO MAKE THE BATTER: In the bowl of a stand mixer fitted with the paddle attachment, add the butter, cane sugar, and vanilla extract. Mix on low until combined and there are no butter chunks.

Add the milk and sour cream and mix on low to combine, scraping down the sides of the bowl to mix in any butter that may stick to the sides.

In a separate bowl, add the cake flour, baking powder, sea salt, and nutmeg and whisk together. With mixer on low, slowly add in the cake flour mixture and mix until you have a smooth batter.

Pour the batter into the prepared baking pan. Bake for 1 hour, or until a toothpick inserted in the center comes out clean. Allow to cool completely in the pan.

TO MAKE THE GLAZE: In a medium bowl, add the powdered sugar and milk and whisk until a smooth glaze forms.

Spread the glaze on top of the loaf cake. Top with rainbow sprinkles.

Store in an airtight container for up to 3 days.

GLUTEN-FREE

Replace the cake flour with a scant 1⅔ cups (248 g) gluten-free flour blend.

HIGH ALTITUDE

Bake at 350°F for 45 minutes, or until a toothpick inserted into the center comes out clean.

ORANGE CARDAMOM LOAF CAKE

MAKES A 1-POUND LOAF CAKE

The subtle spice of cardamom paired with vanilla in this loaf cake creates such an inviting flavor. I top this one with a sweet orange buttercream. This loaf cake pairs well with tea, hot chocolate, and of course a big glass of milk.

BATTER

½ cup (113 g) salted butter, softened

¾ cup (170 g) cane sugar

1 teaspoon vanilla extract

1 cup (237 ml) milk, room temperature

¼ cup (57 g) sour cream, room temperature

1¾ cups (248 g) cake flour

1 teaspoon baking powder

½ teaspoon fine sea salt

½ teaspoon cardamom

FROSTING

1 cup (142 g) powdered sugar, sifted

¼ cup (57 g) salted butter, softened

2 teaspoons orange juice

1 teaspoon orange flavor

Zest of half an orange

Preheat the oven to 350°F. Line a 1-pound loaf pan with parchment paper, letting it fold over the sides for easier removal.

TO MAKE THE BATTER: In the bowl of a stand mixer fitted with the paddle attachment, add the butter, cane sugar, and vanilla extract. Mix on low until combined and there are no butter chunks.

Add the milk and sour cream and mix on low to combine, scraping down the sides of the bowl to mix in any butter that may stick to the sides.

In a separate bowl, add the cake flour, baking powder, sea salt, and cardamom. Whisk together to combine. With the mixer on low, slowly add in the flour mixture and mix until combined and you have a smooth cake batter, scraping down the sides of the bowl as needed.

Pour the batter into the prepared baking pan. Bake for 1 hour, or until a toothpick inserted in the center comes out clean. Allow to cool completely in the pan.

TO MAKE THE FROSTING: In the bowl of a stand mixer fitted with the paddle attachment, add the powdered sugar, butter, orange juice, orange flavor, and orange zest. Mix on low until combined, then speed up the mixer to high for 1 minute, or until light and fluffy.

Spread the frosting on top of the loaf cake.

Store in an airtight container for up to 3 days.

GLUTEN-FREE

Replace the cake flour with a scant 1⅔ cups (248 g) gluten-free flour blend.

HIGH ALTITUDE

Bake at 350°F for 45 minutes, or until a toothpick inserted into the center comes out clean.

BLUEBERRY PISTACHIO LOAF CAKE

MAKES A 1-POUND LOAF CAKE

Blueberry and pistachio is a combination I make often. The sweetness of the blueberries pairs very well with the nuttiness and lightly salty flavor of pistachios. You can easily swap out pistachios for almonds, pecans, or cashews, which would all be equally delicious in different ways. These recipe options mean this is a loaf cake you can make again and again, just a little different each time.

BATTER

¼ cup (35 g) shelled roasted and salted pistachios

1¾ cups (248 g) cake flour

1 teaspoon baking powder

½ teaspoon fine sea salt

½ cup (113 g) salted butter, softened

¾ cup (170 g) cane sugar

1 teaspoon vanilla extract

1 cup (237 ml) milk, room temperature

¼ cup (57 g) vanilla yogurt, room temperature

FROSTING

1½ cups (212 g) powdered sugar, sifted

6 tablespoons (85 g) salted butter, softened

2 tablespoons heavy whipping cream

TOPPING

6 ounces (170 g) blueberries

Preheat the oven to 350°F. Line a 1-pound loaf pan with parchment paper, letting it fold over the sides for easier removal.

TO MAKE THE BATTER: In a food processor, process the pistachios until they are a fine powder. Transfer to a large bowl and add the cake flour, baking powder, and sea salt and whisk together. Set aside.

In the bowl of a stand mixer fitted with the paddle attachment, add the butter, cane sugar, and vanilla extract. Mix on low until combined and there are no butter chunks.

Add the milk and yogurt and mix on low to combine, scraping down the sides of the bowl to mix in any butter that may stick to the sides. With the mixer on low, slowly add in the cake flour mixture and mix until you have a smooth batter.

Pour the batter into the prepared baking pan. Bake for 1 hour, or until a toothpick inserted in the center comes out clean. Allow to cool completely in the pan.

TO MAKE THE FROSTING: In the bowl of a stand mixer fitted with the paddle attachment, add the powdered sugar, butter, and whipping cream. Mix on low until combined, then speed up the mixer to high for 1 minute, or until light and fluffy.

Spread the frosting on top of the loaf cake. Top with the blueberries.

Store in an airtight container in the fridge for up to 3 days.

GLUTEN-FREE

Replace the cake flour with a scant 1⅔ cups (248 g) gluten-free flour blend.

HIGH ALTITUDE

Bake at 350°F for 45 minutes, or until a toothpick inserted into the center comes out clean.

VANILLA CHERRY LOAF CAKE

MAKES A 1-POUND LOAF CAKE

This loaf cake is seriously impressive given how easy it is to make. The fresh cherries on top add a wow factor that is so easy to accomplish! This is the cake to bake when it's cherry season! You can use Bing cherries, like I have here, or you can also use Rainier cherries or tart cherries to make this cake a little different. The many cherry varieties just mean you can make this cake multiple times during cherry season!

BATTER

½ cup (113 g) salted butter, softened

¾ cup (170 g) cane sugar

1 teaspoon vanilla extract

1 cup (237 ml) milk, room temperature

¼ cup (57 g) sour cream, room temperature

1¾ cups (248 g) cake flour

1 teaspoon baking powder

½ teaspoon fine sea salt

CHERRY COMPOTE

4 ounces (113 g) Bing cherries, pitted

2 tablespoons (28 g) cane sugar

¼ cup (59 ml) water

FROSTING

1 cup (142 g) powdered sugar, sifted

¼ cup (57 g) salted butter, softened

2 tablespoons (30 ml) cherry juice (made from the Cherry Compote)

TOPPING

10 ounces (284 g) Bing cherries

Preheat the oven to 350°F. Line a 1-pound loaf pan with parchment paper, letting it fold over the sides for easier removal.

TO MAKE THE BATTER: In the bowl of a stand mixer fitted with the paddle attachment, add the butter, cane sugar, and vanilla extract. Mix on low until combined and there are no butter chunks.

Add the milk and sour cream and mix on low to combine, scraping down the sides of the bowl to mix in any butter that may stick to the sides.

In a separate bowl, add the cake flour, baking powder, and sea salt and whisk together. With mixer on low, slowly add in the cake flour mixture and mix until you have a smooth batter.

Pour the batter into the prepared baking pan. Bake for 1 hour, or until a toothpick inserted in the center comes out clean. Allow to cool completely in the pan.

TO MAKE THE COMPOTE: In a small saucepan, add the cherries, cane sugar, and water. Put over medium heat and stir to combine. The sugar will dissolve into the water and the cherries will start to burst. Allow the mixture to cook until it has reduced by about half, 5 to 10 minutes. Remove from the heat and strain with a strainer so you have the juice. Retain 2 tablespoons of the juice. (Store the extra cherry compote in an airtight container in the fridge and use to top Baked French Toast, page 36, for breakfast!)

TO MAKE THE FROSTING: In the bowl of a stand mixer fitted with the paddle attachment, add the powdered sugar, butter, and cherry juice. Mix on low until combined, then speed up the mixer to high for 1 minute, or until light and fluffy.

Spread the frosting on top of the loaf cake. Top with fresh cherries.

Store in an airtight container in the fridge for up to 3 days.

⊘
GLUTEN-FREE

Replace the cake flour with a
scant 1⅔ cups (248 g) gluten-
free flour blend.

🏔
HIGH ALTITUDE

Bake at 350°F for 45 minutes,
or until a toothpick inserted
into the center comes out
clean.

CHOCOLATE PECAN BABKA

MAKES A 1-POUND LOAF

Babka is one of my favorite brunch recipes. Babka is a sweet yeast bread with swirls of chocolate running through it everywhere; the more the better. Babka is traditionally a Jewish pastry that was created using leftover challah dough filled and swirled to make this sweet pastry. While challah traditionally has eggs, and so does babka, I bet you won't miss them in this recipe!

DOUGH

1 tablespoon (10 g) active dry yeast

¼ cup (57 g) plus ½ teaspoon cane sugar

¼ cup (59 ml) warm water

¼ cup (57 g) salted butter

1 cup (237 ml) milk

1 teaspoon raw honey

3½ cups (446 g) all-purpose flour

1 teaspoon fine sea salt

FILLING

6 ounces (170 g) dark chocolate, chopped

4 tablespoons (57 g) salted butter

½ cup (71 g) powdered sugar, sifted

¾ cup (96 g) pecans, chopped

GLAZE

½ cup (71 g) powdered sugar, sifted

2 tablespoons (30 ml) water

HIGH ALTITUDE

Bake at 350°F for 35 minutes, or until golden brown.

TO MAKE THE DOUGH: In the bowl of a stand mixer fitted with the dough hook, add the yeast, ½ teaspoon cane sugar, and warm water. Stir to combine and let sit for 5 minutes, until bubbly.

In a small pot over medium heat, add the butter, milk, and honey. Stir until completely melted; remove from heat.

Add the flour, remaining ¼ cup cane sugar, and sea salt to the mixing bowl in that order. Add the milk mixture and knead on speed 2 to 4 for 5 minutes.

Place the dough in a greased bowl, cover the bowl with a kitchen towel, and let rise for 2 to 3 hours, until doubled in size.

Preheat the oven to 350°F. Line a 1-pound loaf pan with parchment paper.

TO MAKE THE FILLING: In a small saucepan, add the dark chocolate and butter. Put over medium heat and allow the butter and chocolate to melt completely. Remove from heat and add the powdered sugar and stir to combine completely. Set aside.

On a lightly floured surface, roll out the dough to about 12 by 9 inches. Using a spatula, spread the chocolate filling. Sprinkle the chopped pecans evenly over the filling.

Starting at the shorter side, roll the dough so it is completely rolled into a log. Pinch the dough to seal it and put the seam side down. Using a sharp knife, cut the dough log in half lengthwise to expose the rolled inside. Twist the halves together, leaving the cut side up. Transfer to the prepared loaf pan.

Bake for 40 minutes, or until golden brown. Allow to cool in the pan completely.

TO MAKE THE GLAZE: In a medium bowl, add the powdered sugar and water and whisk together until you have a smooth glaze. Using a pastry brush, brush the glaze over the top of the babka.

Store in an airtight container for up to 3 days.

Cookies

Cookies will always hold a special place in my heart. They were my dessert of choice as a child and they still are today. Cookies were what inspired me to open a bake shop, they were what I built my business on, and they are what I wrote my first book about! So, of course, I must have an entire chapter dedicated to eggless cookies.

Cookies transcend all celebrations, and there isn't a time when cookies are not appropriate. Whether it's a birthday, a Tuesday afternoon, or Christmas— cookies are always welcome. This chapter is complete with all the eggless cookies you could want: soft and chewy cookies, sandwich cookies, short-breads, thumbprints, and more.

There is a cookie for everyone inside this chapter. Some of my favorites are Chocolate Chip Cookies (page 95), Strawberry Thumbprints (page 108), Chocolate-Dipped Shortbreads (page 115), and Chocolate Brownie Cookies (page 103). I also love adding ice cream on top of a Chocolate Peanut Butter Cup Cookie Skillet (page 107)!

CHOCOLATE CHIP COOKIES

MAKES 20 COOKIES

This is the recipe that inspired this whole book! And it's a recipe that is on heavy rotation in my kitchen. There's nothing better than soft, chewy chocolate chip cookies, and these hit all the notes. I whip the butter for a full 5 minutes, which is super important in this recipe. Whipping the butter and sugar aerates the dough, creating little pockets of air that help cookies puff up in the oven. This is especially important for getting that soft and chewy texture for cookies without eggs. If you can't wait for the dough to refrigerate overnight, you're welcome to bake them right away. But you'll be richly rewarded if you can be patient—the long refrigeration time makes the cookies chewier and gives them more flavor.

¾ cup (170 g) salted butter, softened

½ cup (113 g) cane sugar

½ cup (113 g) packed dark brown sugar

1 teaspoon vanilla extract

¼ cup (59 ml) milk

2 cups (255 g) all-purpose flour

½ teaspoon baking soda

½ teaspoon fine sea salt

¾ cup (142 g) semisweet chocolate chips

GLUTEN-FREE

Replace the all-purpose flour with 1¾ cups (269 g) gluten-free flour blend.

HIGH ALTITUDE

Bake at 375°F for 12 to 14 minutes, until lightly browned on the bottom.

Line a baking sheet with parchment paper.

In the bowl of a stand mixer fitted with the paddle attachment, add the butter, cane sugar, brown sugar, and vanilla extract. Mix on low until combined and there are no chunks of butter. Then continue to mix on low for 5 minutes; set a timer. The butter mixture will be light and fluffy.

Add the milk, flour, baking soda, and sea salt in that order and mix on low until a dough forms. Add the chocolate chips and mix on low until combined.

Using your hands or a 2-tablespoon cookie scoop, roll or scoop the dough into 20 balls and place them on the prepared baking sheet. Refrigerate the baking sheet overnight.

Preheat the oven to 375°F. Line a second baking sheet with parchment paper and place the cookie dough balls evenly onto each sheet so there is space between them. Or you can just bake off what you want right now and store the rest of the dough in the fridge (covered in an airtight container) for up to 7 days.

Bake for 13 to 15 minutes, until lightly browned on the bottom.

Store in an airtight container for up to 7 days.

CHEWY OATMEAL RAISIN COOKIES

MAKES 24 COOKIES

To create a perfectly chewy cookie, you just need the right combination of ingredients and method. I whip the butter in these cookies to help create their chewy texture. That chewy texture is enhanced by the use of less flour and the addition of finely shredded coconut. Even though you can barely taste the coconut in these cookies, it's truly necessary for the amazing soft and chewy texture! You can refrigerate the cookie dough for up to 7 days if you don't want to bake them all at once.

½ cup (113 g) salted butter, softened

½ cup (113 g) cane sugar

¼ cup (57 g) packed dark brown sugar

1⅓ cups (170 g) all-purpose flour

1½ teaspoons cinnamon

½ teaspoon baking soda

½ teaspoon fine sea salt

½ cup (118 ml) milk

1 cup plus 2 tablespoons (113 g) rolled oats

⅔ cup (57 g) fine shredded unsweetened coconut

1 cup (155 g) raisins

Preheat the oven to 375°F. Line two baking sheets with parchment paper.

In the bowl of a stand mixer fitted with the paddle attachment, add the butter, cane sugar, and brown sugar. Mix on low until combined and there are no chunks of butter. Continue to mix on low for 5 minutes, until the butter mixture is light and fluffy.

In a separate bowl, add the flour, cinnamon, baking soda, and sea salt and whisk together. Add the milk and flour mixture to the butter mixture and mix on low until combined. Add the oats, coconut, and raisins and mix on low until combined.

Using your hands, form the dough into 24 balls and place on the prepared baking sheets, spacing them at least 1 inch apart. Flatten them slightly so they are about 2 inches in diameter.

Bake for 11 to 14 minutes, until the tops look cracked and set. Allow to cool completely on the baking sheets.

Store in an airtight container for up to 7 days.

GLUTEN-FREE

Use gluten-free oats and replace the all-purpose flour with 1 cup plus 3 tablespoons (184 g) gluten-free flour blend.

HIGH ALTITUDE

Bake at 375°F for 8 to 10 minutes, until the tops look cracked and set.

BAKERY PEANUT BUTTER COOKIES

MAKES 24 COOKIES

These peanut butter cookies are so soft and chewy and have a true peanut butter flavor—they're just like the kind you'd find at your favorite bakery. Peanut butter is an amazing ingredient to use in eggless baking, as it provides flavor and structure. Peanut butter combined with applesauce gives these cookies flavor as well as moisture that would usually be provided by eggs. These cookies are also good for making ice cream sandwiches, as their soft and chewy texture lends perfectly to being frozen along with the ice cream.

½ cup (113 g) salted butter, softened

½ cup (113 g) packed dark brown sugar

½ cup (113 g) cane sugar, plus more for dusting

1 teaspoon vanilla extract

1 cup (226 g) peanut butter

¼ cup (57 g) applesauce

1 cup plus 2 tablespoons (142 g) all-purpose flour

½ teaspoon baking soda

½ teaspoon fine sea salt

Preheat the oven to 375°F. Line two baking sheets with parchment paper.

In the bowl of a stand mixer fitted with the paddle attachment, add the butter, brown sugar, cane sugar, and vanilla extract. Mix on low until combined and there are no chunks of butter.

Add the peanut butter and applesauce and mix for 2 to 4 rotations, just to combine. Add the flour, baking soda, and sea salt in that order and mix on low until combined into a smooth dough. Do not overmix.

Using your hands, form the dough into 24 balls and place on the prepared baking sheets, spacing them at least 1 inch apart. Flatten them slightly so they are about 2 inches in diameter.

Bake for 11 to 14 minutes, until the tops look cracked and set. Sprinkle with cane sugar immediately after coming out of the oven. Allow to cool completely on the baking sheets.

Store in an airtight container for up to 7 days.

GLUTEN-FREE

Replace the all-purpose flour with 1 cup (155 g) gluten-free flour blend.

HIGH ALTITUDE

Bake at 375°F for 8 to 10 minutes, until the tops look cracked and set.

SPICED SNICKERDOODLE COOKIES

MAKES 24 COOKIES

These soft and chewy snickerdoodles are spiced with my favorite spice trio: cinnamon, ginger, and cloves. These make a delicious fall cookie. I even consider these to be holiday snickerdoodles, as the spices just make you feel warm and cozy. I like to enjoy them with a cup of tea or a vanilla steamer.

DOUGH

¾ cup (170 g) salted butter, softened

1 cup (226 g) cane sugar

1 teaspoon vanilla extract

2 cups (255 g) all-purpose flour

1½ teaspoons baking powder

½ teaspoon fine sea salt

½ teaspoon cinnamon

½ teaspoon cloves

½ teaspoon ginger

¼ cup (59 ml) milk

TOPPING

1 tablespoon (28 g) cane sugar

1 teaspoon cinnamon

Preheat the oven to 375°F. Line two baking sheets with parchment paper.

TO MAKE THE DOUGH: In the bowl of a stand mixer fitted with the paddle attachment, add the butter, cane sugar, and vanilla extract. Mix on low until combined, then mix for 5 minutes or until light and fluffy.

In a separate bowl, add the flour, baking powder, sea salt, cinnamon, cloves, and ginger and whisk together. Add the milk and flour mixture to the butter mixture and mix on low until combined.

TO MAKE THE TOPPING: In a small bowl, add the sugar and cinnamon and mix together.

Using your hands, roll the dough into 24 balls and then roll the balls in the topping mixture. Place on the prepared baking sheets, spacing at least 1 inch apart.

Bake for 11 to 14 minutes, until the tops look cracked and set. Allow to cool completely on the baking sheets.

Store in an airtight container for up to 7 days.

GLUTEN-FREE

Replace the all-purpose flour with 1¾ cups (269 g) gluten-free flour blend.

HIGH ALTITUDE

Bake at 375°F for 8 to 10 minutes, until the tops look cracked and set.

CHOCOLATE BROWNIE COOKIES

MAKES 24 COOKIES

I have an affinity for cookies with glaze on top. In fact, they are my all-time fave! This cookie, with all that chocolate, is one I bake all the time. The glaze is best if you can let it set for 24 hours before eating—difficult, I know. But trust me, the wait will make for the best consistency. My trick is I glaze all the cookies at once and then stick the whole baking sheet in the freezer for 24 hours. They set up perfectly, and the cookies stay soft because they are sealed up in the freezer. Just thaw and eat!

DOUGH

½ cup (113 g) salted butter, softened

¾ cup (170 g) cane sugar

1⅔ cups (212 g) all-purpose flour

½ cup (43 g) Dutch cocoa powder, sifted

1½ teaspoons baking powder

½ teaspoon fine sea salt

½ teaspoon ground vanilla bean

½ cup (118 ml) milk

¾ cup (142 g) semisweet chocolate chips

GLAZE

1½ cups (212 g) powdered sugar, sifted

½ cup (43 g) Dutch cocoa powder, sifted

3½ tablespoons (52 ml) milk

Preheat the oven to 375°F. Line two baking sheets with parchment paper.

TO MAKE THE DOUGH: In the bowl of a stand mixer fitted with the paddle attachment, add the butter and cane sugar. Mix on low until combined and there are no chunks of butter.

In a separate bowl, add the flour, cocoa, baking powder, sea salt, and vanilla bean and mix together. Add the milk and flour mixture to the butter mixture and mix on low until combined into a smooth dough. Add the chocolate chips and mix on low to combine completely.

Using your hands, form the dough into 24 balls and place on the prepared baking sheets, spacing them at least 1 inch apart. Flatten them slightly so they are about 2 inches in diameter.

Bake for 11 to 14 minutes, until the tops look cracked and set. Allow to cool completely on the baking sheets.

TO MAKE THE GLAZE: In a medium bowl, add the powdered sugar, cocoa, and milk and whisk until you have a smooth glaze. Using a butter knife or spatula, spread the glaze over the top of each cookie.

Store in an airtight container for up to 7 days.

GLUTEN-FREE

Replace the all-purpose flour with a scant 1½ cups (227 g) gluten-free flour blend.

HIGH ALTITUDE

Bake at 375°F for 8 to 10 minutes, until the tops look cracked and set.

SUGAR COOKIE SKILLET

MAKES A 10-INCH COOKIE SKILLET

There's nothing like a soft-baked vanilla sugar cookie. Some might say it needs to have rainbow sprinkles, some maybe not. You can make this skillet cookie either with or without sprinkles. Regardless, I think it's mandatory to top it with freshly made whipped cream!

DOUGH

½ cup (113 g) salted butter, softened

½ cup (113 g) cane sugar

½ cup (71 g) powdered sugar, sifted

2 teaspoons vanilla extract

½ cup (118 ml) milk

2 cups (255 g) all-purpose flour

1½ teaspoons baking powder

½ teaspoon fine sea salt

½ cup (85 g) rainbow sprinkles (optional)

TOPPING

1 cup (237 ml) heavy whipping cream

1½ teaspoons cane sugar

½ teaspoon vanilla extract

Preheat the oven to 300°F.

TO MAKE THE DOUGH: In the bowl of a stand mixer fitted with the paddle attachment, add the butter, cane sugar, powdered sugar, and vanilla extract. Mix on low until combined and there are no butter chunks.

Add the milk, flour, baking powder, and sea salt in that order. Mix on low until combined into a dough. Add the rainbow sprinkles and mix on low until combined.

Transfer the dough into a 10-inch cast-iron skillet and press it into the bottom and sides so it's evenly distributed.

Bake for 42 to 47 minutes, until the cookie looks set in the middle.

TO MAKE THE TOPPING: In the bowl of a stand mixer fitted with the paddle attachment, add the whipping cream, cane sugar, and vanilla extract. Mix on low and gradually increase the speed as the mixture starts to thicken, until you are at full speed. Whisk until stiff peaks form.

Serve with the fresh whipped cream over the top of the warm cookie skillet.

Store the extra whipped cream in the fridge for up to 3 days and store the cookie in an airtight container for up to 7 days.

GLUTEN-FREE

Replace the all-purpose flour with 1¾ cups (269 g) gluten-free flour blend.

HIGH ALTITUDE

Bake at 300°F for 40 to 44 minutes, until the cookie looks set in the middle.

CHOCOLATE PEANUT BUTTER CUP COOKIE SKILLET

MAKES A 10-INCH COOKIE SKILLET

The best commercially made organic mini peanut butter cups are from Justin's (either milk or dark). That's what I use when I make this cookie skillet, and I eat all the extras while I'm baking it! I love adding coarse sea salt on top of this skillet for a sweet and salty combination. This is completely optional, and even traditional fine sea salt will work too!

½ cup (113 g) salted butter, softened

½ cup (113 g) packed dark brown sugar

¼ cup (57 g) cane sugar

1 teaspoon vanilla extract

½ cup (118 ml) milk

2 cups (255 g) all-purpose flour

½ teaspoon baking soda

½ teaspoon fine sea salt

20 mini peanut butter cups, cut in halves or quarters

Coarse sea salt for topping

Preheat the oven to 300°F.

In the bowl of a stand mixer fitted with the paddle attachment, add the butter, brown sugar, cane sugar, and vanilla extract. Mix on low until combined and no chunks of butter remain.

Add the milk, flour, baking soda, and sea salt in that order. Mix on low until combined into a dough. Add the peanut butter cups and mix on low until combined.

Transfer the dough into a 10-inch cast-iron skillet and press it into the bottom and sides so it's evenly distributed.

Bake for 42 to 47 minutes, until the cookie looks set in the middle. Sprinkle the top with coarse sea salt.

Store in an airtight container for up to 7 days.

GLUTEN-FREE

Replace the all-purpose flour with 1¾ cups (269 g) gluten-free flour blend.

HIGH ALTITUDE

Bake at 300°F for 40 to 44 minutes, until the cookie looks set in the middle.

STRAWBERRY THUMBPRINTS

MAKES 30 COOKIES

This recipe is a great base recipe for a vanilla thumbprint cookie. This particular one uses strawberries, but you can add any kind of jam or preserves that you want. Just switch things up with whatever is in season—blueberry, apricot, raspberry, and more—to make tons of different thumbprint cookies.

DOUGH

1 cup (226 g) salted butter, softened

¾ cup (170 g) cane sugar

1 teaspoon vanilla extract

¼ cup (57 g) cream cheese

3 cups (383 g) all-purpose flour

¼ teaspoon cinnamon

6 ounces (170 g) strawberry preserves

GLAZE

1 cup (142 g) powdered sugar, sifted

2 tablespoons water

GLUTEN-FREE

Replace the all-purpose flour with 2½ cups plus 1 tablespoon (397 g) gluten-free flour blend.

HIGH ALTITUDE

Bake at 350°F for 15 to 19 minutes, until lightly browned on the bottom.

Line two baking sheets with parchment paper.

TO MAKE THE DOUGH: In the bowl of a stand mixer fitted with the paddle attachment, add the butter, cane sugar, and vanilla extract. Mix on low until combined and no chunks of butter remain. Continue to mix on low for an additional 5 minutes, until the mixture looks light and fluffy.

Add the cream cheese and mix to combine completely.

Add the flour and cinnamon and mix until a smooth dough forms.

Using your hands, form the dough into 30 balls and place on the prepared baking sheets, spacing them at least 1 inch apart. Flatten them slightly and press your thumb into the center to create an indent. Fill each indent with strawberry preserves.

Place the baking sheets in the fridge for 30 minutes. Preheat the oven to 350°F.

Bake for 19 to 23 minutes, until lightly browned on the bottom. Allow to cool completely on the baking sheets.

TO MAKE THE GLAZE: In a medium bowl, add the powdered sugar and water and whisk together until a smooth glaze forms. Drizzle over the tops of the cookies.

Store in a cool dry place for up to 7 days.

GRAPE THUMBPRINTS

MAKES 30 COOKIES

I started eating grapes dipped in cream cheese when I was living on my own and would either forget to shop for food or had no money to do so. I ate bagels a lot, so of course cream cheese was always in my fridge. And one of my favorite fruits is grapes, even though they are on the more expensive side of fruits, so I always bought them, even as a broke teenager! This flavor combination might seem strange, but it's a surprisingly delicious one, and I love pairing them together in desserts. These will be a new favorite of yours, I'm sure!

DOUGH

1 cup (226 g) salted butter, softened

¾ cup (170 g) cane sugar

1 teaspoon almond extract

¼ cup (57 g) cream cheese

3 cups (383 g) all-purpose flour

6 ounces (170 g) grape preserves

GLAZE

1 cup (142 g) powdered sugar, sifted

2 tablespoons water

GLUTEN-FREE

Replace the all-purpose flour with 2½ cups plus 1 tablespoon (397 g) gluten-free flour blend.

HIGH ALTITUDE

Bake at 350°F for 15 to 19 minutes, until lightly browned on the bottom.

Line two baking sheets with parchment paper.

TO MAKE THE DOUGH: In the bowl of a stand mixer fitted with the paddle attachment, add the butter, cane sugar, and almond extract. Mix on low until combined and no chunks of butter remain. Continue to mix on low for an additional 5 minutes, until the mixture looks light and fluffy.

Add the cream cheese and mix to combine completely.

Add the flour and mix until a smooth dough forms.

Using your hands, form the dough into 30 balls and place on the prepared baking sheets, spacing them at least 1 inch apart. Flatten them slightly and press your thumb into the center to create an indent. Fill each indent with grape preserves.

Place the baking sheets in the fridge for 30 minutes. Preheat the oven to 350°F.

Bake for 19 to 23 minutes, until lightly browned on the bottom. Allow to cool completely on the baking sheets.

TO MAKE THE GLAZE: In a medium bowl, add the powdered sugar and water and whisk together until a smooth glaze forms. Drizzle over the tops of the cookies.

Store in a cool dry place for up to 7 days.

VANILLA BEAN SHORTBREADS

MAKES 28 COOKIES

There is nothing quite like a classic shortbread cookie. Many shortbread recipes are naturally eggless, but that's not always the case. I use ground vanilla bean in these cookies for a true vanilla flavor, one that is different than vanilla extract. If you can get ground vanilla bean, I highly recommend it! If you have only vanilla extract, substitute 2 teaspoons of vanilla extract in place of the 1 teaspoon of vanilla bean.

1 cup (226 g) salted butter, softened

1 cup (142 g) powdered sugar, sifted

2 cups (255 g) all-purpose flour

1 teaspoon ground vanilla bean

HIGH ALTITUDE

Bake at 350°F for 12 to 14 minutes, until lightly golden brown around the edges.

In the bowl of a stand mixer fitted with the paddle attachment, add the butter and powdered sugar. Mix on low until combined.

Add the flour and vanilla bean and mix on low until combined.

Have a large piece of plastic wrap ready. Roll the dough into a log that is about 12 inches long. Wrap it in plastic wrap and place in the fridge overnight.

Preheat the oven to 350°F. Line two baking sheets with parchment paper.

Cut the log into slices that are about ¼ inch thick and place on the prepared baking sheets.

Bake for 13 to 15 minutes, until lightly golden brown around the edges.

Store in a cool dry place for up to 7 days.

CHOCOLATE-DIPPED SHORTBREADS

MAKES 28 COOKIES

I use kamut flour in these shortbread cookies to give them an interesting and hearty flavor. I highly recommend trying out this specialty flour! It has a nutty and sweet flavor that makes a simple cookie, like shortbread, extra special.

DOUGH

1 cup (226 g) salted butter, softened

1 cup (142 g) powdered sugar, sifted

2 teaspoons vanilla extract

2 cups (310 g) kamut flour

Cane sugar for dusting

TOPPING

10 ounces (284 g) milk chocolate, chopped

HIGH ALTITUDE

Bake at 350°F for 12 to 14 minutes, until lightly golden brown around the edges.

TO MAKE THE DOUGH: In the bowl of a stand mixer fitted with the paddle attachment, add the butter, powdered sugar, and vanilla extract. Mix on low until combined.

Add the flour and mix on low until combined.

Have a large piece of plastic wrap ready. Roll the dough into a log that is about 12 inches long. Wrap it in plastic wrap and place in the fridge overnight.

Preheat the oven to 350°F. Line two baking sheets with parchment paper.

Cut the log into slices that are about ¼ inch thick and place on the prepared baking sheets.

Bake for 13 to 15 minutes, until lightly golden brown around the edges. Sprinkle with cane sugar immediately after coming out of the oven.

TO MAKE THE TOPPING: Using a double boiler, melt about 80 percent of the chocolate until it reaches 110°F on a chocolate thermometer. Remove from heat and add in the remaining 20 percent; stir vigorously to combine. Allow the chocolate to come down to 89°F.

Dip each cookie bottom side down in the milk chocolate and place back on the parchment paper. Place the baking sheet in the fridge to set for at least 1 hour.

Store in a cool dry place, or in the fridge for up to 7 days.

MINT CHOCOLATE SHORTBREADS

MAKES 36 COOKIES

Just like the classic Thin Mints you can buy, these mint chocolate short-breads are dipped in dark chocolate. But these are made with much better ingredients! If you want to coat them completely just like Thin Mints, just double the amount of dark chocolate and dunk the entire cookie instead of just one side!

DOUGH

1 cup (226 g) salted butter, softened

1 cup (142 g) powdered sugar, sifted

2 teaspoons peppermint flavor

1⅔ cups (212 g) all-purpose flour

½ cup (43 g) Dutch cocoa powder, sifted

TOPPING

10 ounces (284 g) dark chocolate, chopped

GLUTEN-FREE

Replace the all-purpose flour with a scant 1⅓ cups (212 g) gluten-free flour blend and ¼ cup plus 1 tablespoon (28 g) coconut flour.

HIGH ALTITUDE

Bake at 350°F for 12 to 14 minutes, until set and dry.

Preheat the oven to 350°F. Line two baking sheets with parchment paper.

TO MAKE THE DOUGH: In the bowl of a stand mixer fitted with the paddle attachment, add the butter, powdered sugar, and peppermint flavor. Mix on low until combined and you no longer see the powdered sugar. There will still be a few chunks of butter, but that is okay because it's very soft.

Add the flour and cocoa into the butter mixture and mix on low until combined and smooth. The dough should feel like play dough in your hands.

Using your hands, form the dough into 36 balls and place them on the prepared baking sheets. Flatten each one slightly so they are about 1¾ inches in diameter.

Bake for 13 to 15 minutes, until they are set and dry. Allow to cool completely on the baking sheets.

TO MAKE THE TOPPING: Using a double boiler, melt about 80 percent of the dark chocolate until it reaches 115°F on a chocolate thermometer. Remove from heat and add in the remaining 20 percent; stir vigorously to combine. Allow the chocolate to come down to 91°F.

Dip each cookie halfway in the dark chocolate and place back on the parchment paper. Place the baking sheet in the fridge to set for at least 1 hour.

Store in a cool dry place or in the fridge for up to 7 days.

OATMEAL CREAM PIES

MAKES 14 SANDWICHES

This is childhood in a cookie—at least for me. These were a coveted brown-bag lunch treat when I was young. Only when I had something really good in my lunch could I trade a classmate for their oatmeal cream pie, as my mom never bought or made them. Now I can make them whenever I want!

DOUGH

½ cup (113 g) salted butter, softened

1 cup (226 g) packed light brown sugar

½ cup (113 g) applesauce

1½ cups (191 g) all-purpose flour

1 cup plus 2 tablespoons (113 g) rolled oats

1 teaspoon cinnamon

½ teaspoon baking soda

½ teaspoon fine sea salt

FILLING

Heaping 2⅓ cups (340 g) powdered sugar, sifted

¼ cup (57 g) salted butter, softened

½ cup (118 ml) heavy whipping cream

Preheat the oven to 375°F. Line two baking sheets with parchment paper.

TO MAKE THE DOUGH: In the bowl of stand mixer fitted with the paddle attachment, add the butter and brown sugar. Mix on low until combined and there are no chunks of butter.

Add the applesauce, flour, oats, cinnamon, baking soda, and sea salt in that order. Mix on low until combined into a stiff dough.

Using your hands, form into 28 balls and place on prepared baking sheets about 1 inch apart.

Bake for 11 to 14 minutes, until the tops look set. Allow to cool completely on the baking sheets.

TO MAKE THE FILLING: In the bowl of a stand mixer fitted with the paddle attachment, add the powdered sugar, butter, and heavy whipping cream. Mix on low until combined, then speed up the mixer to high and mix for 1 minute, or until light and fluffy.

Using a spatula or knife, top every other cookie with the filling and sandwich two of them together.

Store in an airtight container in the fridge for up to 3 days.

GLUTEN-FREE

Use gluten-free oats and replace the all-purpose flour with a heaping 1¼ cups (205 g) gluten-free flour blend.

HIGH ALTITUDE

Bake at 375°F for 8 to 10 minutes, until the tops look cracked and set.

LEMON COOKIE PIES

MAKES 12 SANDWICHES

Sweet, tart, and zesty—these extra soft and chewy cookie pies are bursting
with lemon flavor! You can mix it up and get a slightly different lemon flavor
by using traditional lemons or Meyer lemons when they are in season.

DOUGH

½ cup (113 g) salted butter,
softened

1 cup (142 g) powdered sugar,
sifted

½ cup (113 g) cane sugar

2 teaspoons lemon flavor

½ cup (118 ml) milk

2 cups (255 g) all-purpose
flour

1½ teaspoons baking powder

½ teaspoon fine sea salt

Zest of half a lemon

FILLING

3 cups (425 g) powdered
sugar, sifted

¾ cup (170 g) salted butter,
softened

2 tablespoons lemon juice

GLUTEN-FREE

Replace the all-purpose flour
with 1¾ cups (269 g) gluten-free
flour blend.

HIGH ALTITUDE

Bake at 375°F for 8 to
10 minutes, until the tops look
cracked and set.

Preheat the oven to 375°F. Line two baking sheets with parchment
paper.

TO MAKE THE DOUGH: In the bowl of stand mixer fitted with the
paddle attachment, add the butter, powdered sugar, cane sugar,
and lemon flavor. Mix on low until combined and there are no
chunks of butter.

Add the milk, flour, baking powder, sea salt, and lemon zest in that
order. Mix on low until combined into a dough and no bits of flour
remain. Refrigerate dough for 15 to 20 minutes, until it's not too
sticky.

Using your hands, form the dough into 24 balls and place on the
prepared baking sheets about 1 inch apart. Flatten them slightly so
they are about 2 inches in diameter.

Bake for 11 to 14 minutes, until the tops look cracked and set. Allow
to cool completely on the baking sheets.

TO MAKE THE FILLING: In the bowl of a stand mixer fitted with the
paddle attachment, add the powdered sugar, butter, and lemon
juice. Mix on low until combined, then speed up the mixer to high
and mix for 1 minute, or until light and fluffy. Transfer to a piping
bag with Ateco tip #864.

Pair up the cookies and pipe a swirl of the filling onto every other
cookie, then sandwich them together.

Store in an airtight container in the fridge for up to 3 days.

BROWN SUGAR COOKIE PIES

MAKES 12 SANDWICHES

Cookie pies are my name for those soft, thin, melt-in-your-mouth kind of sandwich cookies. My *yiayia* (grandma in Greek) used to bring me a similar-style cookie from her favorite grocery bakery. When she walked in the door with a brown bag in her hand, I knew I was in for a treat! These will always be a favorite of mine.

DOUGH

½ cup (113 g) salted butter, softened

1 cup (226 g) packed dark brown sugar

½ cup (118 ml) milk

2 cups (255 g) all-purpose flour

½ teaspoon fine sea salt

½ teaspoon baking soda

FILLING

2 cups (284 g) powdered sugar, sifted

4 tablespoons salted butter, softened

2 tablespoons (30 ml) milk

GLUTEN-FREE

Replace the all-purpose flour with 1¾ cups (269 g) gluten-free flour blend.

HIGH ALTITUDE

Bake at 375°F for 8 to 10 minutes, until the tops look cracked and set.

Preheat the oven to 375°F. Line two baking sheets with parchment paper.

TO MAKE THE DOUGH: In the bowl of stand mixer fitted with the paddle attachment, add the butter and brown sugar. Mix on low until combined and there are no chunks of butter.

Add the milk, flour, sea salt, and baking soda in that order. Mix on low until combined into a stiff dough.

Using your hands, form the dough into 24 balls and place on the prepared baking sheets about 1 inch apart. Flatten them slightly so they are about 2 inches in diameter.

Bake for 11 to 14 minutes, until the tops look cracked and set. Allow to cool completely on the baking sheets.

TO MAKE THE FILLING: In the bowl of a stand mixer fitted with the paddle attachment, add the powdered sugar, butter, and milk. Mix on low until combined, then speed up the mixer to high and mix for 1 minute, or until light and fluffy.

Using a spatula or knife, top every other cookie with the filling and sandwich two of them together.

Store in an airtight container in the fridge for up to 3 days.

ORANGE CREAM SANDWICH COOKIES

MAKES 18 SANDWICHES

Light and creamy, these sandwich cookies are buttery, crisp, and bursting with sweet orange flavor. They're filled with an extra creamy buttercream for a true cream center. I always bake these for the nonchocolate lovers in my life, like my brother!

DOUGH

1 cup (226 g) salted butter, softened

1 cup (142 g) powdered sugar, sifted

2 teaspoons orange flavor

2 cups (255 g) all-purpose flour

Zest of 1 orange

FILLING

1½ cups plus 1 tablespoon (226 g) powdered sugar, sifted

½ cup (113 g) salted butter, softened

1 to 2 teaspoons heavy whipping cream

GLUTEN-FREE

Replace the all-purpose flour with a scant 1½ cups (226 g) gluten-free flour blend and ½ cup plus 1 tablespoon (57 g) coconut flour.

HIGH ALTITUDE

Bake at 350°F for 12 to 14 minutes, until lightly browned on the bottoms.

Preheat the oven to 350°F. Line two baking sheets with parchment paper.

TO MAKE THE DOUGH: In the bowl of a stand mixer fitted with the paddle attachment, add the butter, powdered sugar, and orange flavor. Mix on low until combined.

Add the flour and orange zest and mix on low until a smooth dough forms; it should feel like play dough in your hands.

Using your hands, form the dough into 36 balls and place on the prepared baking sheets, spacing at least 1 inch apart. Flatten them slightly so they are about 1¾ inches in diameter.

Bake for 13 to 15 minutes, until lightly browned on the bottoms. Allow to cool completely on the baking sheets.

TO MAKE THE FILLING: In the bowl of a stand mixer fitted with the paddle attachment, add the powdered sugar, butter, and cream. Mix on low until combined, then speed up the mixer to high for 1 minute, or until light and fluffy. Transfer to a piping bag with no tip.

Pair the cookies together by size and turn over every other cookie. Pipe a dollop of filling onto each turned-over cookie and sandwich them together.

Store in a cool dry place for up to 7 days.

CHOCOLATE PEANUT BUTTER SANDWICH COOKIES

MAKES 18 SANDWICHES

Everyone's favorite pairing—chocolate and peanut butter! I use a decorating tip to give these cookies a little bit of cuteness. But if you don't have a decorating tip, no worries! They'll taste equally delicious.

DOUGH

1 cup (226 g) salted butter, softened

1 cup (142 g) powdered sugar, sifted

2 teaspoons vanilla extract

1⅔ cups (212 g) all-purpose flour

½ cup (43 g) Dutch cocoa powder, sifted

FILLING

1½ cups plus 1 tablespoon (226 g) powdered sugar, sifted

½ cup (113 g) salted butter, softened

2 tablespoons (32 g) peanut butter

2 to 3 teaspoons milk

½ teaspoon vanilla extract

GLUTEN-FREE

Replace the all-purpose flour with a scant 1⅓ cups (212 g) gluten-free flour blend and ¼ cup plus 1 tablespoon (28 g) coconut flour.

HIGH ALTITUDE

Bake at 350°F for 12 to 14 minutes, until set and dry.

Preheat the oven to 350°F. Line two baking sheets with parchment paper.

TO MAKE THE DOUGH: In the bowl of a stand mixer fitted with the paddle attachment, add the butter, powdered sugar, and vanilla extract. Mix on low until combined.

Add the flour and cocoa and mix on low until a smooth dough forms; it should feel like play dough in your hands.

Using your hands, form the dough into 36 balls and place on the prepared baking sheets, spacing at least 1 inch apart. Flatten them slightly so they are about 1¾ inches in diameter.

Bake for 13 to 15 minutes, until set and dry. Allow to cool completely on the baking sheets.

TO MAKE THE FILLING: In the bowl of a stand mixer fitted with the paddle attachment, add the powdered sugar, butter, peanut butter, milk, and vanilla extract. Mix on low until combined, then speed up the mixer to high for 1 minute, or until light and fluffy. Transfer to a piping bag with Ateco tip #864.

Pair the cookies together by size and turn over every other cookie. Pipe a swirl of filling onto each turned-over cookie and sandwich them together.

Store in a cool dry place for up to 7 days.

TOASTED COCONUT ALMOND SANDWICH COOKIES

MAKES 18 SANDWICHES

These light and summery cookies pair perfectly with a scoop of vanilla bean ice cream for a summertime treat. The toasted coconut is also a treat all itself. I always toast extra coconut when I make this recipe, as I like to have it on hand for topping granola, yogurt, smoothie bowls, and more. If you make some extra toasted coconut, just be sure to store it in an airtight container.

DOUGH

1 cup (226 g) salted butter, softened

1 cup (142 g) powdered sugar, sifted

2 teaspoons almond extract

2 cups (255 g) all-purpose flour

FILLING

⅓ cup (28 g) fine shredded unsweetened coconut

Heaping 2⅓ cups (340 g) powdered sugar, sifted

¾ cup (170 g) salted butter, softened

1 to 2 teaspoons coconut milk

1 teaspoon coconut extract

GLUTEN-FREE

Replace the all-purpose flour with a scant 1½ cups (226 g) gluten-free flour blend and ½ cup plus 1 tablespoon (57 g) coconut flour.

HIGH ALTITUDE

Bake at 350°F for 12 to 14 minutes, until lightly browned on the bottoms.

Preheat the oven to 350°F. Line two baking sheets with parchment paper.

TO MAKE THE DOUGH: In the bowl of a stand mixer fitted with the paddle attachment, add the butter, powdered sugar, and almond extract. Mix on low until combined.

Add the flour and mix on low until a smooth dough forms; it should feel like play dough in your hands.

Using your hands, form the dough into 36 balls and place on the prepared baking sheets, spacing them at least 1 inch apart. Flatten them slightly so they are about 1¾ inches in diameter.

Bake for 13 to 15 minutes, until lightly browned on the bottoms. Allow to cool completely on the baking sheets.

TO MAKE THE FILLING: Line a baking sheet with parchment paper. Add the coconut and bake for 5 minutes, or until lightly browned.

In the bowl of a stand mixer fitted with the paddle attachment, add the powdered sugar, butter, coconut milk, and coconut extract. Mix on low until combined, then speed up the mixer to high for 1 minute, or until light and fluffy. Transfer to a piping bag with no tip.

Add the toasted coconut to a shallow bowl. Pair the cookies together by size and turn over every other cookie. Pipe a dollop of filling onto each turned-over cookie, sandwich them together, and roll the middle of the cookies into the toasted coconut to coat the exposed filling.

Store in a cool dry place for up to 7 days.

Bars & Biscotti

Bars are probably the most versatile recipes because you can enjoy them for breakfast, as snacks, or even for dessert. I'm not going to lie, I love having Chocolate Chip Biscotti (page 154) with some coconut water in the morning. I also like making Peanut Butter Honey Blondies (page 137) for a midmorning snack before a hike.

Bars are great for on-the-go snacks. They can easily be wrapped up to take with you anywhere. A tip for getting perfectly cut bars every time: After they have cooled, pop the pan in the fridge for 15 to 20 minutes before removing. Chilling the bars a little helps you remove them from the pan easily, without breakage. As a result, you'll get nice, clean cuts and perfect-looking bars.

Brownies, blondies, and biscotti are all desserts that traditionally contain eggs. When making eggless versions of these desserts, having a good pan is crucial. The same goes for baking sheets for making biscotti. I use the same size pan, 9-inch square, for all the bar recipes in this chapter. I highly recommend that you use a USA PAN product when you bake eggless desserts, as the little ridges of the pan will really help your bars bake evenly and rise properly, which is something eggs are responsible for in traditional bars.

DARK CHOCOLATE FUDGY BROWNIES

MAKES 9 BROWNIES

Contrary to what you may think, brownies are actually more chewy and fudgy without eggs! As I mentioned in the beginning of the book, egg whites are mostly water, which can dry out baked goods. In other words, brownies can become drier and more cakey with egg whites in the mix. This is typically why chewy brownies contain only egg yolks when using eggs. I use chocolate milk in this recipe for an extra creamy chocolate flavor and for added moisture and fat, which is what egg yolks offer. I also add cornstarch to hold these brownies together, as eggs act as a binder in baked goods and cornstarch can mimic that.

¾ cup (170 g) cane sugar

½ cup (113 g) packed dark brown sugar

2 ounces (57 g) dark chocolate, chopped

⅔ cup (57 g) Dutch cocoa powder

½ cup (118 ml) boiling water

½ cup (118 ml) canola oil

¼ cup (59 ml) chocolate milk

1⅓ cups (212 g) all-purpose flour

2 teaspoons cornstarch

½ teaspoon baking powder

½ teaspoon fine sea salt

½ teaspoon ground vanilla bean

Preheat the oven to 350°F. Line a 9-by-9-inch baking pan with parchment paper.

In the bowl of a stand mixer fitted with the paddle attachment, add the cane sugar, brown sugar, dark chocolate, cocoa, and boiling water and mix on low until the chocolate and cocoa have completely melted together with the sugar; there should be no chunks of chocolate.

Add the canola oil, chocolate milk, flour, cornstarch, baking powder, sea salt, and vanilla bean in that order and mix on low until combined. Do not overmix. Transfer to the prepared baking pan.

Bake for 20 to 25 minutes, until a toothpick inserted in the center comes out clean. Allow to cool completely in the baking pan.

Cut into nine brownies.

Store in an airtight container for up to 5 days.

GLUTEN-FREE

Replace the all-purpose flour with a scant 1⅓ cups (212 g) gluten-free flour blend.

HIGH ALTITUDE

Bake at 350°F for 18 to 23 minutes, until a toothpick inserted in the center comes out clean.

CARDAMOM CHOCOLATE CHIP BROWNIES

MAKES 9 BROWNIES

These brownies are on the cakey side, and they pair perfectly with a big glass of milk. The trick to getting a good cakey brownie is having a higher flour-to-fat ratio. You still need moisture (that eggs would normally bring), and that's done here by adding chocolate milk, which adds even more chocolate flavor.

½ cup (113 g) salted butter, melted

¾ cup (170 g) cane sugar

2 tablespoons (44 g) maple syrup

2 cups (255 g) all-purpose flour

½ cup (43 g) Dutch cocoa powder, sifted

½ teaspoon ground vanilla bean

½ teaspoon baking powder

½ teaspoon fine sea salt

¼ teaspoon cardamom

½ cup (118 ml) chocolate milk

¼ cup (59 ml) heavy whipping cream

¾ cup (142 g) semisweet chocolate chips

Preheat the oven to 350°F. Line a 9-by-9-inch baking pan with parchment paper.

In the bowl of a stand mixer fitted with the paddle attachment, add the melted butter, cane sugar, and maple syrup and mix together until combined.

In a separate bowl, add the flour, cocoa, ground vanilla bean, baking powder, sea salt, and cardamom and whisk together. Add the chocolate milk, heavy whipping cream, and flour mixture to the butter mixture and mix on low until combined.

Add the chocolate chips and mix to combine completely. Transfer to the prepared baking pan and spread evenly.

Bake for 30 to 35 minutes, until a toothpick inserted in the center comes out clean. Allow to cool completely in the baking pan.

Cut into nine brownies.

Store in an airtight container for up to 5 days.

GLUTEN-FREE

Replace the all-purpose flour with 1⅔ cups (255 g) gluten-free flour blend.

HIGH ALTITUDE

Bake at 350°F for 25 to 30 minutes, until a toothpick inserted in the center comes out clean.

PEANUT BUTTER HONEY BLONDIES

MAKES 9 BLONDIES

Sweet and a little bit salty, these blondies hit all the notes. With their soft and extra chewy texture, you'll want to make these again and again! These are best when served with a glass of milk.

½ cup (113 g) salted butter, melted

½ cup (113 g) packed dark brown sugar

¼ cup (57 g) cane sugar

1 teaspoon vanilla extract

½ cup plus 2 tablespoons (142 g) peanut butter

½ cup (118 ml) milk

¼ cup (59 ml) heavy whipping cream

2 tablespoons (43 g) raw honey

2 cups (255 g) all-purpose flour

½ teaspoon baking powder

½ teaspoon fine sea salt

Preheat the oven to 350°F. Line a 9-by-9-inch baking pan with parchment paper.

In the bowl of a stand mixer fitted with the paddle attachment, add the melted butter, brown sugar, cane sugar, and vanilla extract. Mix on low until combined.

Add the peanut butter, milk, cream, honey, flour, baking powder, and sea salt in that order. Mix on low until combined; do not over-mix. Transfer the batter to the prepared baking dish and spread evenly.

Bake for 30 to 35 minutes, until a toothpick inserted in the center comes out clean. Allow to cool completely in the pan.

Cut into nine squares. Store in an airtight container for up to 5 days.

GLUTEN-FREE

Replace the all-purpose flour with 1⅔ cups (255 g) gluten-free flour blend.

HIGH ALTITUDE

Bake at 350°F for 25 to 30 minutes, until a toothpick inserted in the center comes out clean.

CHOCOLATE CHIP BLONDIES

MAKES 9 BLONDIES

There's nothing better than a soft and gooey blondie filled with chocolate chips. I use cashew butter in this recipe for a subtly sweet flavor that gives these blondies all the texture of a traditional blondie made with eggs.

½ cup (113 g) salted butter, melted

½ cup (113 g) cane sugar

¼ cup (57 g) packed light brown sugar

1 teaspoon vanilla extract

½ cup plus 2 tablespoons (142 g) cashew butter

1 tablespoon (22 g) maple syrup

½ cup (118 ml) milk

¼ cup (59 ml) heavy whipping cream

2 cups (255 g) all-purpose flour

½ teaspoon baking powder

½ teaspoon fine sea salt

¾ cup (142 g) semisweet chocolate chips

Preheat the oven to 350°F. Line a 9-by-9-inch baking pan with parchment paper.

In the bowl of a stand mixer fitted with the paddle attachment, add the melted butter, cane sugar, brown sugar, and vanilla extract. Mix on low until combined.

Add the cashew butter, maple syrup, milk, whipping cream, flour, baking powder, and sea salt in that order. Mix on low until combined and you don't see any flour bits.

Add the chocolate chips and mix to combine completely.

Transfer the batter to the baking pan and spread evenly.

Bake for 30 to 35 minutes, until a toothpick inserted in the center comes out clean. Allow to cool completely in the pan.

Cut into nine squares. Store in an airtight container for up to 5 days.

GLUTEN-FREE

Replace the all-purpose flour with 1⅔ cups (255 g) gluten-free flour blend.

HIGH ALTITUDE

Bake at 350°F for 25 to 30 minutes, until a toothpick inserted in the center comes out clean.

BLISS BARS

MAKES 9 BARS

Transporting you into pure bliss! These bars are perfect for anytime snacking. You can even switch up the dried fruit and nuts, using whatever you have on hand to make these a little different every time. Other combos I enjoy are dried blueberries and almonds, and dried strawberries and hazelnuts.

DOUGH

½ cup (113 g) salted butter, softened

½ cup (113 g) cane sugar

¼ cup (57 g) packed light brown sugar

½ teaspoon orange flavor

½ cup (118 ml) milk

2 cups (255 g) all-purpose flour

½ teaspoon baking soda

½ teaspoon fine sea salt

Zest of 1 orange

1 cup (127 g) dried cranberries

1 cup (113 g) walnuts, chopped

TOPPING

4 ounces (113 g) white chocolate, chopped

Preheat the oven to 325°F. Line a 9-by-9-inch baking pan with parchment paper.

TO MAKE THE DOUGH: In the bowl of a stand mixer fitted with the paddle attachment, add the butter, cane sugar, brown sugar, and orange flavor. Mix on low until combined and no chunks of butter remain.

Add the milk, flour, baking soda, sea salt, and orange zest in that order. Mix on low until a dough forms. Add the cranberries and walnuts and mix on low until combined.

Press the dough evenly into the prepared pan.

Bake for 30 to 34 minutes, until a toothpick inserted in the center comes out clean. Allow to cool completely.

TO MAKE THE TOPPING: In a double boiler, melt the white chocolate completely. Drizzle over the top of the bars.

Remove the bars from the pan and cut into nine squares.

Store in an airtight container for up to 7 days.

GLUTEN-FREE

Replace the all-purpose flour with 1¾ cups (269 g) gluten-free flour blend.

HIGH ALTITUDE

Bake at 325°F for 26 to 30 minutes, until a toothpick inserted in the center comes out clean.

SUGAR COOKIE BARS

MAKES 16 BARS

Soft and chewy just like your favorite sugar cookies but in a square bar. I prefer to cut these into 16 bars, as I like them more bite-sized, but you can also cut them into nine bars for a larger serving. This is an easy recipe to dress up for any holiday—simply swap out the rainbow sprinkles for any type of festive sprinkles. They make a great addition to holiday cookie boxes!

DOUGH

½ cup (113 g) salted butter, softened

¾ cup (170 g) cane sugar

½ cup (71 g) powdered sugar, sifted

¼ cup (57 g) cream cheese

1 teaspoon vanilla extract

¼ cup (59 ml) milk

2¼ cups (284 g) all-purpose flour

1½ teaspoons baking powder

½ teaspoon fine sea salt

¼ teaspoon cinnamon

FROSTING

2 cups (284 g) powdered sugar, sifted

½ cup (113 g) salted butter, softened

1 tablespoon (15 ml) milk

Rainbow sprinkles

Preheat the oven to 325°F. Line a 9-by-9-inch baking pan with parchment paper.

TO MAKE THE DOUGH: In the bowl of a stand mixer fitted with the paddle attachment, add the butter, cane sugar, powdered sugar, cream cheese, and vanilla extract. Mix on low until combined and no chunks of butter remain.

Add the milk, flour, baking powder, sea salt, and cinnamon in that order. Mix on low until a dough forms.

Press the dough evenly into the prepared pan.

Bake for 30 to 34 minutes, until a toothpick inserted in the center comes out clean. Allow to cool completely.

TO MAKE THE FROSTING: In the bowl of a stand mixer fitted with the paddle attachment, add the powdered sugar, butter, and milk and mix on low until combined. Speed up the mixer to high for 1 minute, or until light and fluffy.

Remove the bars from the pan, spread the frosting on top, and top with rainbow sprinkles. Cut into 16 bars.

Store in an airtight container for up to 7 days.

GLUTEN-FREE

Replace the all-purpose flour with 1¾ cups plus 3 tablespoons (297 g) gluten-free flour blend.

HIGH ALTITUDE

Bake at 325°F for 26 to 30 minutes, until a toothpick inserted in the center comes out clean.

CHOCOLATE COCONUT BARS

MAKES 9 BARS

Chocolate and coconut is the pairing that sparked my baking obsession. I built my whole business on my Dad's Coconut Chocolate Chip recipe, and I make new coconut and chocolate desserts anytime I can! These bars are perfect for any time of day.

DOUGH

½ cup (113 g) salted butter, softened

¾ cup (170 g) cane sugar

1 teaspoon coconut extract

½ cup (118 ml) coconut milk

2 cups (255 g) all-purpose flour

⅔ cup (57 g) fine shredded unsweetened coconut

1½ teaspoons baking powder

½ teaspoon fine sea salt

TOPPING

⅓ cup (28 g) fine shredded unsweetened coconut

FROSTING

1 cup (142 g) powdered sugar, sifted

¼ cup (57 g) salted butter, softened

⅓ cup (28 g) Dutch cocoa powder, sifted

2 tablespoons (30 ml) coconut milk

Preheat the oven to 325°F. Line a 9-by-9-inch baking pan with parchment paper.

TO MAKE THE DOUGH: In the bowl of a stand mixer fitted with the paddle attachment, add the butter, cane sugar, and coconut extract. Mix on low until combined and no chunks of butter remain.

Add the coconut milk, flour, coconut, baking powder, and sea salt in that order. Mix on low until a dough forms.

Press the dough evenly into the prepared pan.

Bake for 30 to 34 minutes, until a toothpick inserted in the center comes out clean. Allow to cool completely.

TO MAKE THE TOPPING: Line a baking sheet with parchment paper and spread out the coconut. Toast for 3 to 5 minutes, until golden brown.

TO MAKE THE FROSTING: In the bowl of a stand mixer fitted with the paddle attachment, add the powdered sugar, butter, cocoa, and coconut milk and mix on low until combined. Speed up the mixer to high for 1 minute, or until light and fluffy.

Remove the bars from the pan, spread the frosting on top, and sprinkle with the toasted coconut. Cut into nine bars.

Store in an airtight container for up to 7 days.

GLUTEN-FREE

Replace the all-purpose flour with 1¾ cups (269 g) gluten-free flour blend.

HIGH ALTITUDE

Bake at 325°F for 26 to 30 minutes, until a toothpick inserted in the center comes out clean.

PANTRY BARS

MAKES 16 TRIANGLES

I love creating recipes that I can customize and add literally anything. And these bars are exactly that! What do you have in your pantry? You can use anything you want inside this delicious cookie bar. Feel free to swap out the chocolate chips for milk chocolate, dark chocolate, or white chocolate, the potato chips for pretzels, or the peanuts and raisins for any kind of dried fruits or nuts you may have. I bet you'll come up with something creative and delicious!

½ cup (113 g) salted butter, softened

½ cup (113 g) cane sugar

¼ cup (57 g) packed dark brown sugar

1 teaspoon vanilla extract

½ cup (118 ml) milk

2 cups (255 g) all-purpose flour

½ teaspoon baking soda

½ teaspoon fine sea salt

¾ cup (142 g) semisweet chocolate chips

⅔ cup (100 g) roasted and salted peanuts

½ cup (77 g) raisins

2 cups (43 g) potato chips

Coarse sea salt for topping

Preheat the oven to 325°F. Line a 9-by-9-inch baking pan with parchment paper.

In the bowl of a stand mixer fitted with the paddle attachment, add the butter, cane sugar, brown sugar, and vanilla extract. Mix on low until combined and no chunks of butter remain.

Add the milk, flour, baking soda, and sea salt in that order. Mix on low until a dough forms. Add the chocolate chips, peanuts, raisins, and potato chips and mix on low until combined.

Press the dough evenly into the prepared pan.

Bake for 30 to 34 minutes, until a toothpick inserted in the center comes out clean. Sprinkle with coarse sea salt immediately after they come out of the oven. Allow to cool completely.

Remove the bars from the pan and cut into 16 triangles.

Store in an airtight container for up to 7 days.

GLUTEN-FREE

Replace the all-purpose flour with 1¾ cups (269 g) gluten-free flour blend.

HIGH ALTITUDE

Bake at 325°F for 26 to 30 minutes, until a toothpick inserted in the center comes out clean.

GINGERBREAD BARS

MAKES 9 BARS

Gingerbread isn't just for the holidays. The magical trio of spices that makes up gingerbread is cinnamon, cloves, and ginger. Some people add nutmeg or cardamom, but I truly believe that all you need are the magic three! I like to enjoy gingerbread all year-round. When I bite into this soft and chewy gingerbread bar, it just transports me to my favorite time of year, and then I feel all warm and cozy no matter what month it is.

DOUGH

½ cup (113 g) salted butter, softened

½ cup (113 g) packed dark brown sugar

¼ cup (57 g) cane sugar

3 tablespoons (57 g) blackstrap molasses

¼ cup (59 ml) milk

¼ cup (57 g) applesauce

2 cups (255 g) all-purpose flour

1 teaspoon cinnamon

1 teaspoon cloves

1 teaspoon ginger

½ teaspoon baking soda

½ teaspoon fine sea salt

FROSTING

1½ cups (212 g) powdered sugar, sifted

6 tablespoons (85 g) salted butter, softened

2 tablespoons (30 ml) milk

½ teaspoon vanilla extract

Preheat the oven to 325°F. Line a 9-by-9-inch baking pan with parchment paper.

TO MAKE THE DOUGH: In the bowl of a stand mixer fitted with the paddle attachment, add the butter, brown sugar, cane sugar, and molasses. Mix on low until combined and no chunks of butter remain.

Add the milk, applesauce, flour, cinnamon, cloves, ginger, baking soda, and sea salt in that order. Mix on low until a dough forms.

Press the dough evenly into the prepared pan.

Bake for 30 to 34 minutes, until a toothpick inserted in the center comes out clean. Allow to cool completely.

TO MAKE THE FROSTING: In the bowl of a stand mixer fitted with the paddle attachment, add the powdered sugar, butter, milk, and vanilla extract and mix on low until combined. Speed up the mixer to high for 1 minute, or until light and fluffy.

Remove the bars from the pan and spread the frosting on top. Cut into nine bars.

Store in an airtight container for up to 7 days.

GLUTEN-FREE

Replace the all-purpose flour with 1¾ cups (269 g) gluten-free flour blend.

HIGH ALTITUDE

Bake at 325°F for 26 to 30 minutes, until a toothpick inserted in the center comes out clean.

ALMOND BISCOTTI

MAKES 12 BISCOTTI

Almond biscotti are so classic. My mom made them every year for Christmas, and it wasn't until I was older that I truly appreciated the subtle but sweet flavor of this biscotti. Now they're one of my favorites. While biscotti are technically cookies, they're bar-like because of their long shape. Making biscotti without eggs is very similar to making eggless cookies. I find that milk is a great egg substitute, as milk brings fat and flavor!

½ cup (113 g) salted butter, softened

¾ cup (170 g) cane sugar

1 teaspoon almond extract

⅓ cup (71 g) almond butter

2 cups (255 g) all-purpose flour

1½ teaspoons baking powder

½ teaspoon fine sea salt

1 cup (142 g) whole almonds with their skins, roughly chopped

½ cup (118 ml) milk

GLUTEN-FREE

Replace the all-purpose flour with 1¾ cups (269 g) gluten-free flour blend.

HIGH ALTITUDE

Bake at 350°F for 30 minutes, or until the middle looks set but not completely done, then remove and let rest for 10 minutes. Cut as instructed and bake again for 15 minutes.

Preheat the oven to 350°F. Line a baking sheet with parchment paper.

In the bowl of a stand mixer fitted with the paddle attachment, add the butter, cane sugar, and almond extract. Mix on low until combined and there are no chunks of butter.

In a separate bowl, add the flour, baking powder, sea salt, and chopped almonds and mix together.

Add the milk and the flour mixture to the butter mixture and mix on low until combined into a stiff dough.

Using your hands, form the cookie dough into a large log and flatten it slightly so it's about 1 inch thick; it should be about 13 by 3 inches.

Bake for 35 minutes, or until the middle looks set but not completely done. Remove from the oven and let rest for 10 minutes. Trim off the edges, then slice into 12 pieces and bake again for 20 minutes. Allow to cool completely on the baking sheet.

Store in a cool dry place for up to 7 days.

LEMON POPPY SEED BISCOTTI

MAKES 12 BISCOTTI

The classic flavor combination of lemon and poppy seeds never gets old. These buttery, crisp, and sweet biscotti are a recipe you'll want to make during citrus season, when lemons are fresh and flavorful!

½ cup (113 g) salted butter, softened

¾ cup (170 g) cane sugar, plus 2 tablespoons (28 g) for topping

2 teaspoons lemon flavor

2 cups (255 g) all-purpose flour

1 tablespoon (10 g) poppy seeds

1½ teaspoons baking powder

½ teaspoon fine sea salt

Zest of 1 lemon

⅓ cup (78 ml) milk

2 tablespoons (29 ml) lemon juice

GLUTEN-FREE

Replace the all-purpose flour with 1¾ cups (269 g) gluten-free flour blend.

HIGH ALTITUDE

Bake at 350°F for 30 minutes, or until the middle looks set but not completely done, then remove and let rest for 10 minutes. Cut as instructed and bake again for 15 minutes.

Preheat the oven to 350°F. Line a baking sheet with parchment paper.

In the bowl of a stand mixer fitted with the paddle attachment, add the butter, ¾ cup cane sugar, and lemon flavor. Mix on low until combined and there are no chunks of butter.

In a separate bowl, add the flour, poppy seeds, baking powder, sea salt, and lemon zest and whisk together.

Add the milk, lemon juice, and the flour mixture to the butter mixture and mix on low until combined into a stiff dough.

Using your hands, form the cookie dough into a large log and flatten it slightly so it's about 1 inch thick; it should be about 13 by 3 inches. Sprinkle the top with the remaining 2 tablespoons of cane sugar.

Bake for 35 minutes, or until the middle looks set but not completely done. Remove from the oven and let rest for 10 minutes. Trim off the edges, then slice into 12 pieces and bake again for 20 minutes. Allow to cool completely on the baking sheet.

Store in a cool dry place for up to 7 days.

CHOCOLATE CHIP BISCOTTI

MAKES 12 BISCOTTI

Chocolate chip biscotti is a crowd-pleasing recipe, and it's one I bake often. I knew I had to create an eggless version that was just as good, and this one does not disappoint! They're best when served with a big glass of milk for dipping.

½ cup (113 g) salted butter, softened

¼ cup plus 2 tablespoons (85 g) cane sugar

¼ cup plus 2 tablespoons (85 g) packed dark brown sugar

1 teaspoon vanilla extract

2¼ cups (284 g) all-purpose flour

½ teaspoon baking soda

½ teaspoon fine sea salt

½ cup (118 ml) milk

¾ cup (142 g) semisweet chocolate chips

GLUTEN-FREE

Replace the all-purpose flour with 1¾ cups plus 3 tablespoons (297 g) gluten-free flour blend.

HIGH ALTITUDE

Bake at 350°F for 30 minutes, or until the middle looks set but not completely done, then remove and let rest for 10 minutes. Cut as instructed and bake again for 15 minutes.

Preheat the oven to 350°F. Line a baking sheet with parchment paper.

In the bowl of a stand mixer fitted with the paddle attachment, add the butter, cane sugar, brown sugar, and vanilla extract. Mix on low until combined and there are no chunks of butter.

In a separate bowl, add the flour, baking soda, and sea salt and mix together.

Add the milk and the flour mixture to the butter mixture and mix on low until combined into a stiff dough. Add the chocolate chips and mix on low to combine.

Using your hands, form the cookie dough into a large log and flatten it slightly so it's about 1 inch thick; it should be about 13 by 3 inches.

Bake for 35 minutes, or until the middle looks set but not completely done. Remove from the oven and let rest for 10 minutes. Trim off the edges, then slice into 12 pieces and bake again for 20 minutes. Allow to cool completely on the baking sheet.

Store in a cool dry place for up to 7 days.

HONEY WALNUT BISCOTTI

These biscotti are extra light and sweet. The addition of applesauce gives them an amazing light and crispy texture that is a little different than traditional biscotti. Serve these with chamomile tea on a cozy fall night.

½ cup (113 g) salted butter, softened

½ cup (113 g) cane sugar, plus 2 tablespoons (28 g) for the topping

2 tablespoons (43 g) raw honey

1 teaspoon vanilla extract

2 cups (255 g) all-purpose flour

½ teaspoon baking soda

½ teaspoon fine sea salt

¼ teaspoon cinnamon

¼ cup (59 ml) milk

2 tablespoons (28 g) applesauce

1 cup (113 g) walnuts, chopped

GLUTEN-FREE

Replace the all-purpose flour with 1¾ cups (269 g) gluten-free flour blend.

HIGH ALTITUDE

Bake at 350°F for 30 minutes, or until the middle looks set but not completely done, then remove and let rest for 10 minutes. Cut as instructed and bake again for 15 minutes.

Preheat the oven to 350°F. Line a baking sheet with parchment paper.

In the bowl of a stand mixer fitted with the paddle attachment, add the butter, ½ cup cane sugar, honey, and vanilla extract. Mix on low until combined and there are no chunks of butter.

In a separate bowl, add the flour, baking soda, sea salt, and cinnamon and mix together.

Add the milk, applesauce, and the flour mixture to the butter mixture and mix on low until combined into a smooth dough. Add the walnuts and mix on low to combine.

Using your hands, form the cookie dough into a large log and flatten it slightly so it's about 1 inch thick; it should be about 13 by 3 inches. Sprinkle the top with the remaining 2 tablespoons cane sugar.

Bake for 35 minutes, or until the middle looks set but not completely done. Remove from the oven and let rest for 10 minutes. Trim off the edges, then slice into 12 pieces and bake again for 20 minutes. Allow to cool completely on the baking sheet.

Store in a cool dry place for up to 7 days.

DOUBLE CHOCOLATE BISCOTTI

MAKES 12 BISCOTTI

This is one of my favorite recipes in the whole book! I love chocolate, and these biscotti are up there with my favorite chocolate desserts. Tempering the chocolate isn't necessary here, but it gives it a more professional finish, which is desirable if you plan to gift it. I usually skip the tempering step and just melt all the chocolate in a double boiler, as I prefer to keep these biscotti in the fridge for a cool treat. My other tip is to store these in the fridge in a loaf pan (as opposed to a plate), as it holds all the crumbs!

½ cup (113 g) salted butter, softened

½ cup (113 g) cane sugar

¼ cup (57 g) packed dark brown sugar

1⅔ cups (212 g) all-purpose flour

⅔ cup (57 g) Dutch cocoa powder, sifted

1½ teaspoons baking powder

½ teaspoon fine sea salt

½ teaspoon ground vanilla bean

½ cup (118 ml) chocolate milk

1¾ cups (248 g) chopped milk chocolate for topping

GLUTEN-FREE

Replace the all-purpose flour with a scant 1½ cups (227 g) gluten-free flour blend.

HIGH ALTITUDE

Bake at 350°F for 30 minutes, or until the middle looks set but not completely done, then remove and let rest for 10 minutes. Cut as instructed and bake again for 15 minutes.

Preheat the oven to 350°F. Line a baking sheet with parchment paper.

In the bowl of a stand mixer fitted with the paddle attachment, add the butter, cane sugar, and brown sugar. Mix on low until combined and there are no chunks of butter.

In a separate bowl, add the flour, cocoa, baking powder, sea salt, and vanilla bean and mix together.

Add the chocolate milk and the flour mixture to the butter mixture and mix on low until combined into a stiff dough.

Using your hands, form the cookie dough into a large log and flatten it slightly so it's about 1 inch thick; it should be about 13 by 3 inches.

Bake for 35 minutes, or until the middle looks set but not completely done. Remove from the oven and let rest for 10 minutes. Trim off the edges, then slice into 12 pieces and bake again for 20 minutes. Allow to cool completely on the baking sheet.

Using a double boiler, add 80 percent of the chopped milk chocolate and melt until it reaches 115°F on a chocolate thermometer. Remove from heat and add in the remaining 20 percent of chocolate, then stir to combine completely. Place on a bag of ice to stop the heating process for a minute or so; remove and allow the chocolate to come down to 91°F.

Dip one side of the biscotti into the chocolate and place back on the parchment paper. Place the baking sheet in the fridge for at least 30 minutes to set the chocolate.

Store in a cool dry place for up to 7 days.

Pies & Tarts

Pies and tarts were foreign desserts to me for a very long time. While I was growing up, they were desserts that were reserved for Thanksgiving and Christmas, and that was it. Because they were so unfamiliar to me, pies and tarts were always a little intimidating: Not only had I never made them, but I really didn't eat them very often either. When I opened my bake shop, a local restaurant reached out and asked me if I would bake pies for them, as they wanted a dessert menu but didn't have a pastry chef. Of course, I said yes! But then I had to give myself a crash course in pie baking. Turns out, pies and tarts are actually some of the easiest desserts to make!

So I am here to encourage you to dive into this chapter with moxie. If pies or tarts have ever intimidated you before, fear no more. While tarts may seem pristine, and therefore difficult, I assure you my recipes are very simple. And that's part of what I love about them—you can make an incredibly impressive dessert with little effort!

Meanwhile, pies are rustic and free-form, making them the perfect treat to throw together for a holiday or just a cozy fall day. They do not have to be pristine, and they always taste amazing. It's time to impress your egg-eating friends with pies and tarts that don't use eggs. Typically egg wash is brushed on top of traditional pie flavors like apple, blueberry, and strawberry. Or eggs are used inside a custard filling to set a pie, such as pecan or pumpkin. Eggs are also used in custard pies and tarts, such as cheesecakes.

But in this chapter, you will find creative recipes that don't require eggs. You'll even find a Pie Wash recipe (page 163) that will allow you to make any fruit pie from your family recipe box with a golden-brown crust that's egg-free. If in doubt, start with the Rainbow Fruit Cheesecake Tart (page 180) or the Peanut Butter S'More Tart (page 178)—I'm positive no one will even miss the eggs.

heavy whipping
cream

milk

coconut oil

melted butter

coconut milk

honey + water

PIE WASH

If you are a pie lover, then you probably know that most pies are topped with an egg wash. This wash is either just egg or egg mixed with water. This is typically how a pie crust gets its golden-brown color and shiny look. So you may be wondering how eggless pies can get that golden-brown color. Do not worry; you can still achieve an amazing golden-brown pie crust without eggs!

OPTION 1

2 tablespoons (30 ml) milk

OPTION 2

2 tablespoons (30 ml) heavy whipping cream

OPTION 3

2 tablespoons (28 g) butter, melted

OPTION 4

2 tablespoons (30 ml) coconut milk

OPTION 5

2 tablespoons (28 g) coconut oil, melted

OPTION 6

1 tablespoon (15 ml) honey
1 tablespoon (15 ml) water

This recipe is a substitute for egg wash. You can actually use six different ingredients in place of eggs, and as you can see from the photo, the result is still a crust that looks golden brown! Some are a little more golden brown than others, and some taste a little different. Regardless, any of these eggless washes will help your pie get that golden-brown color in the oven.

You can use whichever option you prefer or whatever ingredient you have on hand. I usually go with milk, as it's easy to just pull out of the fridge and I always have milk on hand. And I also think milk gives the most neutral flavor. My favorite is actually the honey and water option though. This creates the darkest golden brown, as you can see, and it has a very unique flavor that I absolutely love. If you love honey, then this is your new pie wash! The honey and water option does make the pie crust a little sweeter than all the others. If you don't want the honey flavor shining through, then opt for something else. No matter what you choose, they all taste delicious, and they will all brown your pie in the oven. Anywhere in the book that I call for a pie wash, just use whatever option you prefer.

Using a pastry brush, brush over the top of the raw pie dough before baking.

Make sure to coat every nook and cranny for that perfectly golden-brown pie crust!

Bake pie as instructed in the recipe.

STRAWBERRY BASIL MINI PIES

MAKES 6 MINI PIES

I love strawberry and basil together. This sweet and savory combination is something I love creating in desserts, as it brings balance to the sweetness. This recipe is perfect for summertime, when you have in-season strawberries and fresh basil; their true flavors really shine through.

CRUST

2 cups (255 g) all-purpose flour

½ teaspoon cane sugar

¾ cup (170 g) salted butter, cold

½ cup (118 ml) cold water

Pie Wash (page 163)

FILLING

½ cup (113 g) cane sugar

3 tablespoons (21 g) all-purpose flour

1 teaspoon cornstarch

Pinch of fine sea salt

15 ounces (425 g) strawberries, de-stemmed and quartered

TOPPING

6 to 8 fresh basil leaves, finely chopped

HIGH ALTITUDE

Bake at 350°F for 45 to 50 minutes, until golden brown.

TO MAKE THE CRUST: In the bowl of a stand mixer fitted with the paddle attachment, add the flour and cane sugar. Turn on low for two to three rotations to combine the dry ingredients.

Remove the butter from the fridge, cut the stick into four pieces, and then chop into small cubes from there. The smaller the cubes, the flakier the crust. Add the cold cubed butter to the flour mixture. Measure out the cold water and have it ready.

Turn the mixer on low and slowly start to incorporate the ingredients. Gradually turn the mixer to medium speed. Once the butter mixture looks like wet sand, immediately add in all the cold water. As soon as the dough comes together, stop the mixer.

Have six pieces of plastic wrap ready. Divide the dough into six pieces, weighing about 3 ounces (85 g) each. Form each piece of dough into a disk and wrap in plastic wrap. Allow to cool in the fridge for at least 4 hours or overnight before rolling out the pies.

Preheat the oven to 350°F. Line two baking sheets with parchment paper. Have the pie wash ready.

TO MAKE THE FILLING: In a large bowl, add the cane sugar, flour, cornstarch, and sea salt and whisk together. Add the strawberries and toss to coat completely.

Remove the plastic wrap from the six dough disks and place them on a floured surface. Roll out to ¼ inch thick, about 7 inches in diameter. Transfer them to the prepared baking sheets.

Place a generous amount of filling into the middle of each dough, leaving about a 1-inch border. Fold the border into the middle to create a crust. Using a pastry brush, brush the crust of each mini pie with the pie wash.

Bake for 50 to 55 minutes, until golden brown. Let cool completely on the baking sheets. Top with fresh basil before serving.

Store in a cool dry place for up to 3 days.

BLUEBERRY MINI PIES

MAKES 6 MINI PIES

Blueberry pie is my absolute favorite pie. I always add a little bit of cinnamon into the filling, as it brings out the blueberry flavor even more. You can explore other creative flavors in this dessert too. For example, try the honey and water pie wash—its flavor complements the blueberry so well! It's my favorite way to make these mini pies.

CRUST

2 cups (255 g) all-purpose flour

½ teaspoon cane sugar

¾ cup (170 g) salted butter, cold

½ cup (118 ml) cold water

Pie Wash (page 163)

FILLING

½ cup (113 g) cane sugar

3 tablespoons (21 g) all-purpose flour

1 teaspoon cornstarch

½ teaspoon cinnamon

Pinch of fine sea salt

15 ounces (425 g) fresh blueberries

TOPPING

Powdered sugar (optional)

HIGH ALTITUDE

Bake at 350°F for 45 to 50 minutes, until golden brown.

TO MAKE THE CRUST: In the bowl of a stand mixer fitted with the paddle attachment, add the flour and cane sugar. Turn on low for two to three rotations to combine the dry ingredients.

Remove the butter from the fridge, cut the stick into four pieces, and then chop into small cubes from there. The smaller the cubes, the flakier the crust. Add the cold cubed butter to the flour mixture. Measure out the cold water and have it ready.

Turn the mixer on low and slowly start to incorporate the ingredients. Gradually turn the mixer to medium speed. Once the butter mixture looks like wet sand, immediately add in all the cold water. As soon as the dough comes together, stop the mixer.

Have six pieces of plastic wrap ready. Divide the dough into six pieces, weighing about 3 ounces (85 g) each. Form each piece of dough into a disk and wrap in plastic wrap. Allow to cool in the fridge for at least 4 hours or overnight before rolling out the pies.

Preheat the oven to 350°F. Line two baking sheets with parchment paper. Have the pie wash ready.

TO MAKE THE FILLING: In a large bowl, add the cane sugar, flour, cornstarch, cinnamon, and sea salt and whisk together. Add the blueberries and toss to coat completely.

Remove the plastic wrap from the six dough disks and place them on a floured surface. Roll out to ¼ inch thick, about 7 inches in diameter. Transfer them to the prepared baking sheets.

Place a generous amount of filling into the middle of each dough, leaving about a 1-inch border. Fold the border into the middle to create a crust. Using a pastry brush, brush the crust of each mini pie with the pie wash.

Bake for 50 to 55 minutes, until golden brown. Let cool completely on the baking sheets. Sift powdered sugar on top before serving (optional).

Store in a cool dry place for up to 3 days.

CRANBERRY APPLE MINI PIES

MAKES 6 MINI PIES

These mini pies are the perfect addition to any holiday dessert spread. They are individually sized, a little different than your traditional apple pie, and absolutely delicious. I highly recommend using the honey and water pie wash, as it enhances the flavor of the pies and melds beautifully with the apple and spice!

CRUST

2 cups (255 g) all-purpose flour

½ teaspoon cane sugar

¾ cup (170 g) salted butter, cold

½ cup (118 ml) cold water

Pie Wash (page 163)

FILLING

½ cup (113 g) cane sugar

3 tablespoons (21 g) all-purpose flour

1 teaspoon cornstarch

1 teaspoon cinnamon

¼ teaspoon cloves

Pinch of fine sea salt

2 large Fuji apples

5 ounces (142 g) cranberries

GLAZE

1 cup (142 g) powdered sugar, sifted

2 tablespoons (30 ml) water

HIGH ALTITUDE

Bake at 350°F for 45 to 50 minutes, until golden brown.

TO MAKE THE CRUST: In the bowl of a stand mixer fitted with the paddle attachment, add the flour and cane sugar. Turn the mixer on low for two to three rotations to combine the dry ingredients.

Remove the butter from the fridge, cut the stick into four pieces, and then chop into small cubes from there. The smaller the cubes, the flakier the crust. Add the cold cubed butter to the flour mixture. Measure out the cold water and have it ready.

Turn the mixer on low and slowly start to incorporate the butter. Gradually turn the mixer to medium speed. Once the butter mixture looks like wet sand, immediately add in all the cold water. As soon as the dough comes together, stop the mixer.

Have six pieces of plastic wrap ready. Divide the dough into six pieces, weighing about 3 ounces (85 g) each. Form each piece of dough into a disk and wrap in plastic wrap. Allow to cool in the fridge for at least 4 hours or overnight before rolling out the pies.

Preheat the oven to 350°F. Line two baking sheets with parchment paper. Have the pie wash ready.

TO MAKE THE FILLING: In a large bowl, add the cane sugar, flour, cornstarch, cinnamon, cloves, and sea salt and whisk together. Slice the apples into thin slices (leaving skins on). Add the apples and cranberries to the sugar mixture and toss to coat completely.

Remove the plastic wrap from the six dough disks and place them on a floured surface. Roll out to ¼ inch thick, about 7 inches in diameter. Transfer them to the prepared baking sheets.

Place a generous amount of filling into the middle of each dough, leaving about a 1-inch border. Fold the border into the middle to create a crust. Using a pastry brush, brush the crust of each mini pie with the pie wash.

Bake for 50 to 55 minutes, until golden brown. Let cool completely on the baking sheets.

TO MAKE THE GLAZE: In a medium bowl, add the powdered sugar and water and whisk together until you have a smooth glaze. Drizzle over the tops of the pies.

Store in a cool dry place for up to 3 days.

RASPBERRY HAND PIES

MAKES 5 HAND PIES

I like to use raspberry preserves in the middle of these hand pies, as it's an easy way to make them accessible and flavorful all year-round—there's no need to wait for raspberry season!

CRUST

2 cups (255 g) all-purpose flour

½ teaspoon cane sugar

¾ cup (170 g) salted butter, cold

½ cup (118 ml) cold water

Pie Wash (page 163)

FILLING

6 ounces (170 g) raspberry preserves

2 tablespoons (30 ml) water

HIGH ALTITUDE

Bake at 350°F for 45 to 50 minutes, until golden brown

TO MAKE THE CRUST: In the bowl of a stand mixer fitted with the paddle attachment, add the flour and cane sugar. Turn on low for two to three rotations to combine the dry ingredients.

Remove the butter from the fridge, cut the stick into four pieces, and then chop into small cubes from there. The smaller the cubes, the flakier the crust. Add the cold cubed butter to the flour mixture. Measure out the ½ cup cold water and have it ready.

Turn the mixer on low and slowly start to incorporate the ingredients. Gradually turn the mixer to medium speed. Once the butter mixture looks like wet sand, immediately add in all the cold water. As soon as the dough comes together, stop the mixer.

Form the dough into a disk and wrap in plastic wrap. Allow to cool in the fridge for at least 6 hours or overnight before rolling out the pies.

Line a baking sheet with parchment paper.

Remove the plastic wrap from the dough and place on a floured surface. Roll out to ¼ inch thick. Using a 4½-inch cookie cutter or pastry cutter, cut out 10 circles and transfer 5 of them to the prepared baking sheet. Have the water ready in a small dish.

TO MAKE THE FILLING AND ASSEMBLE: Add about 1½ tablespoons raspberry preserves onto the middle of each circle on the parchment paper, leaving a small border. Using your hand, dip your finger into the water and go around the border of one of the pie circles. Then immediately place one of the additional dough circles on top, using the water to seal it together. Repeat with the rest of the pies so each is topped.

Place the baking sheet in the fridge for 15 to 20 minutes, until the dough is firm. Preheat the oven to 350°F. Have the pie wash ready.

Remove the baking sheet from the fridge and, using a fork, crimp the edges around each pie. Brush each pie with the pie wash and make one vent hole in the middle.

Bake for 50 to 55 minutes, until golden brown. Let cool completely on the baking sheet.

Store in a cool dry place for up to 3 days.

CHOCOLATE HAND PIES

MAKES 5 HAND PIES

When the movie *It's Complicated* came out, Meryl Streep's character inspired me even more to become a baker. The scene where she and Steve Martin make chocolate croissants in her bakery after hours will forever be one of my favorite movie scenes. This recipe is what I would have made if I was in that scene. These amazing hand pies are filled with bittersweet chocolate ganache, and the donut-like glaze on top just puts them over the edge.

DOUGH

2 cups (255 g) all-purpose flour

½ teaspoon cane sugar

¾ cup (170 g) salted butter, cold

½ cup (118 ml) cold water

FILLING

2 ounces (57 g) milk chocolate, chopped

2 ounces (57 g) dark chocolate, chopped

¼ cup (59 ml) heavy whipping cream

2 tablespoons (30 ml) water

GLAZE

½ cup (71 g) powdered sugar, sifted

2 tablespoons (30 ml) water

HIGH ALTITUDE

Bake at 350°F for 45 to 50 minutes, until golden brown.

TO MAKE THE DOUGH: In the bowl of a stand mixer fitted with the paddle attachment, add the flour and cane sugar. Turn on low for two to three rotations to combine the dry ingredients.

Remove the butter from the fridge, cut the stick into four pieces, and then chop into small cubes from there. The smaller the cubes, the flakier the crust. Add the cold cubed butter to the flour mixture. Measure out the ½ cup cold water and have it ready.

Turn the mixer on low and slowly start to incorporate the ingredients. Gradually turn the mixer to medium speed. Once the butter mixture looks like wet sand, immediately add in all the cold water. As soon as the dough comes together, stop the mixer.

Form the dough into a disk and wrap in plastic wrap. Allow to cool in the fridge for at least 6 hours or overnight before rolling out the pies.

Line a baking sheet with parchment paper.

TO MAKE THE FILLING: Using a double boiler, add the milk chocolate and dark chocolate and melt completely. Slowly add the cream and whisk until it is completely combined. Remove from heat and allow to set for at least 4 hours, until firm.

Remove the plastic wrap from the dough and place on a floured surface. Roll out to ¼ inch thick. Using a 4½-inch cookie cutter or pastry cutter, cut out 10 circles and transfer 5 of them to the prepared baking sheet. Have the water ready in a small dish.

Add about 1½ tablespoons chocolate filling onto the middle of each circle on the parchment paper, leaving a small border. Using your hand, dip your finger into the water and go around the border of one of the pie circles. Then immediately place one of the additional dough circles on top, using the water to seal it together. Repeat with the rest of the pies so each one is topped.

Place the baking sheet in the fridge for 15 to 20 minutes, until the dough is firm. Preheat the oven to 350°F.

Remove the baking sheet from the fridge and, using a fork, crimp the edges around each pie and make one vent hole in the middle.

Bake for 50 to 55 minutes, until golden brown. Let cool completely on the baking sheet.

TO MAKE THE GLAZE: In a medium bowl, add the powdered sugar and water and whisk together until you have a smooth glaze. Using a pastry brush, brush the tops of each hand pie with the glaze. Allow to set completely before serving.

Store in a cool dry place for up to 3 days.

GLAZED PEACH HAND PIES

MAKES 5 HAND PIES

When peaches are in season, this is the pie recipe to make! I use fresh peach preserves and add my own little twist by adding a touch of cinnamon. You can make your own peach preserves or buy a jar. Either way, these hand pies are amazing! The sweet glaze that covers this entire handheld pie really gives it a pastry-like allure but without all the added time it takes to make pastries.

DOUGH

2 cups (255 g) all-purpose flour

½ teaspoon cane sugar

¾ cup (170 g) salted butter, cold

½ cup (118 ml) cold water

FILLING

6 ounces (170 g) peach preserves

½ teaspoon cinnamon

2 tablespoons (30 ml) water

GLAZE

½ cup (71 g) powdered sugar, sifted

2 tablespoons (30 ml) water

HIGH ALTITUDE

Bake at 350°F for 45 to 50 minutes, until golden brown.

TO MAKE THE DOUGH: In the bowl of a stand mixer fitted with the paddle attachment, add the flour and cane sugar. Turn on low for two to three rotations to combine the dry ingredients.

Remove the butter from the fridge, cut the stick into four pieces, and then chop into small cubes from there. The smaller the cubes, the flakier the crust. Add the cold cubed butter to the flour mixture. Measure out the ½ cup cold water and have it ready.

Turn the mixer on low and slowly start to incorporate the ingredients. Gradually turn the mixer to medium speed. Once the butter mixture looks like wet sand, immediately add in all the cold water. As soon as the dough comes together, stop the mixer.

Form the dough into a disk and wrap in plastic wrap. Allow to cool in the fridge for at least 6 hours or overnight before rolling out the pies.

Line a baking sheet with parchment paper.

TO MAKE THE FILLING: In a medium bowl, mix together the peach preserves and the cinnamon. Have the water ready in a small dish.

Remove the plastic wrap from the dough and place on a floured surface. Roll out to ¼ inch thick. Using a 4½-inch cookie cutter or pastry cutter, cut out 10 circles and transfer 5 of them to the prepared baking sheet.

Add about 1½ tablespoons peach filling onto the middle of each circle on the parchment paper, leaving a small border. Using your hand, dip your finger into the water and go around the border of one of the pie circles. Then immediately place one of the additional dough circles on top, using the water to seal it together. Repeat with the rest of the pies so each is topped.

Place the baking sheet in the fridge for 15 to 20 minutes, until the dough is firm. Preheat the oven to 350°F.

Remove the baking sheet from the fridge and, using a fork, crimp the edges around each pie and make one vent hole in the middle.

Bake for 50 to 55 minutes, until golden brown. Let cool completely on the baking sheets.

TO MAKE THE GLAZE: In a medium bowl, add the powdered sugar and water and whisk together until you have a smooth glaze. Using a pastry brush, brush the tops of each hand pie. Allow to set completely before serving.

Store in a cool dry place for up to 3 days.

MIXED BERRY TART

MAKES A 9½-INCH TART

This easy tart is perfect for any summer night. I use my Vanilla Bean Shortbreads (page 112) here to make an amazing homemade crust! You can use any kind of fresh berries you have on hand. For variations, try blackberries, mulberries, cherries, nectarines, peaches, or whatever summer fruit is in season.

CRUST

18 (340 g) Vanilla Bean Shortbreads (page 112)

6 tablespoons (85 g) salted butter, softened

3 tablespoons (43 g) cane sugar

FILLING

8 ounces (226 g) cream cheese

¼ cup (35 g) powdered sugar, sifted

1 cup (237 ml) heavy whipping cream

1½ teaspoons cane sugar

½ teaspoon vanilla extract

TOPPING

6 ounces (170 g) blueberries

6 ounces (170 g) raspberries

6 ounces (170 g) strawberries, de-stemmed and sliced

HIGH ALITITUDE

Bake at 350°F for 8 to 10 minutes, until lightly golden brown.

TO MAKE THE CRUST: Preheat the oven to 350°F. In a food processor, add the shortbread cookies, butter, and cane sugar. Pulse to combine, then process until combined and uniform.

Transfer the crust to a 9½-inch tart pan and spread evenly. Using your hands, form the crust into the sides of the pan first, working your way all the way around. Then press the remaining shortbread mixture into the bottom of the tart pan, creating an even layer.

Bake for 10 to 12 minutes, until lightly golden brown. Allow to cool completely in the pan.

TO MAKE THE FILLING: In the bowl of a stand mixer fitted with the paddle attachment, add the cream cheese and powdered sugar. Mix on low until combined. Transfer to a bowl and set aside.

In the bowl of a stand mixer fitted with the whisk attachment, add the whipping cream, cane sugar, and vanilla extract. Mix on low, then gradually increase the speed as the whipped cream starts to thicken. Whisk until stiff peaks form.

Add half the whipped cream into the bowl with the cream cheese mixture and fold to combine completely. Transfer to the tart pan and spread evenly.

Transfer the remaining whipped cream to a piping bag with Ateco tip #864.

TO TOP THE TART: Use a mix of blueberries, raspberries, strawberries, and the remaining whipped cream to cover the top of the tart. Get creative!

Store in the fridge for up to 3 days.

PEANUT BUTTER S'MORE TART

MAKES A 9½-INCH TART

This s'more tart is filled with a peanut butter milk chocolate ganache, topped with a marshmallow cream, and torched to perfection. Many people make marshmallows with egg whites; however, this recipe is free of eggs and still has a light and fluffy torched topping! No matter the time of year, when you're craving a s'more and there's no campfire in sight, bake up this easy and impressive tart to enjoy.

CRUST

1½ sleeves (204 g) honey graham crackers, crushed

½ cup (113 g) salted butter, softened

¼ cup plus 1 tablespoon (71 g) cane sugar

FILLING

12 ounces (340 g) milk chocolate, chopped

2 tablespoons (32 g) peanut butter

¾ cup (177 ml) heavy whipping cream

TOPPING

1½ teaspoons (5 g) gelatin

2 tablespoons cold water

½ cup (113 g) cane sugar

¼ cup (78 g) light corn syrup

2 tablespoons warm water

Pinch of fine sea salt

1 cup (142 g) powdered sugar, sifted

GLUTEN-FREE

Use gluten-free graham crackers. Make sure to weigh them to 204 grams, as gluten-free graham crackers usually come in different sizes.

TO MAKE THE CRUST: Preheat the oven to 350°F. In a food processor, add the graham crackers, butter, and cane sugar. Pulse until completely combined and there are no bits of graham cracker or chunks of butter and the mixture is uniform.

Transfer to a 9½-inch tart pan and spread evenly. Using your hands, form the crust into the sides of the pan first, working your way all the way around. Then press the remaining graham cracker mixture into the bottom of the tart pan, creating an even layer.

Bake for 5 to 7 minutes, or until lightly golden brown. Remove from the oven and let cool completely before filling.

TO MAKE THE FILLING: Using a double boiler, add the milk chocolate and peanut butter. Stir frequently and melt completely. Slowly add in the cream and stir until it is completely combined. Transfer to the crust and spread evenly. Allow to set for at least 4 hours.

TO MAKE THE TOPPING: In the bowl of a stand mixer fitted with the whisk attachment, add the gelatin and cold water. Stir to combine completely. Set aside.

In a small saucepan, add the cane sugar, corn syrup, warm water, and sea salt. Put over high heat and stir to combine completely.

Cook until the mixture starts to bubble and rise up, 3 to 5 minutes; remove from heat. Pour over the gelatin mixture and whisk, starting on low and then gradually increasing the speed as the mixture starts to thicken and turn white. Continue to increase the speed until you are on high, then whisk until the mixture has turned bright white and it doesn't fall off the whisk. The whole mixing process should take about 10 minutes.

Add the powdered sugar into the marshmallow cream and whisk to combine completely. Spread over the top of the chocolate filling, leaving a small border of chocolate around the sides.

Torch to your liking with a kitchen torch. Serve immediately.

RAINBOW FRUIT CHEESECAKE TART

MAKES A 9½-INCH TART

If you love cheesecake but haven't been able to enjoy it because of eggs, then this tart is the next best thing! The cheesecake flavor is created with cream cheese, sugar, and heavy whipping cream. The eggless filling has a light and creamy texture that you're sure to love. It's hard to tell the difference between it and traditional cheesecake! This tart is perfect for those summer months when you want a cool dessert that is loaded with fresh fruit.

CRUST

1½ sleeves (204 g) honey graham crackers, crushed

½ cup (113 g) salted butter, softened

¼ cup plus 1 tablespoon (71 g) cane sugar

FILLING

8 ounces (226 g) cream cheese

¼ cup (35 g) powdered sugar, sifted

1 tablespoon lemon juice

Zest of half a lemon

½ cup (118 ml) heavy whipping cream

½ teaspoon vanilla extract

TOPPING

6 ounces (170 g) raspberries

Slices of 1 orange

¼ cup (50 g) diced pineapple

Half a kiwi, sliced

¼ cup (43 g) blueberries

¼ cup (43 g) blackberries

TO MAKE THE CRUST: Preheat the oven to 350°F. In a food processor, add the graham crackers, butter, and cane sugar. Pulse until completely combined and there are no bits of graham cracker or chunks of butter and the mixture is uniform.

Transfer to a 9½-inch tart pan and spread evenly. Using your hands, form the crust into the sides of the pan first, working your way all the way around. Then press the remaining graham cracker mixture into the bottom of the tart pan, creating an even layer.

Bake for 5 to 7 minutes, or until lightly golden brown. Remove from the oven and let cool completely before filling.

TO MAKE THE FILLING: In the bowl of a stand mixer fitted with the paddle attachment, add the cream cheese, powdered sugar, lemon juice, and lemon zest. Mix on low to combine and then speed up the mixer to high and mix for 1 minute, until fluffy. Transfer to a separate bowl and set aside.

In the bowl of a stand mixer fitted with the whisk attachment, add the heavy whipping cream and vanilla extract. Mix on low and gradually increase speed as the mixture starts to thicken until you are at full speed. Whisk until stiff peaks form.

Transfer the whipped cream to the bowl with the cream cheese mixture and fold together. Spread into the tart crust evenly.

Top with fruit, starting at the outside and working your way in. First, place raspberries around the edge, then orange slices, then pineapple, then kiwi, then blueberries and blackberries.

Store in the fridge for up to 3 days.

DARK CHOCOLATE SEA SALT TART

MAKES A 9½-INCH TART

Rich and decadent, this tart will satisfy all your chocolate cravings! I add a coarse flaky sea salt on top to cut a little bit of the richness. If you don't have a coarse sea salt, fine sea salt will work too.

CRUST

1½ sleeves (204 g) honey graham crackers, crushed

½ cup (113 g) salted butter, softened

¼ cup plus 1 tablespoon (71 g) cane sugar

⅓ cup (28 g) Dutch cocoa powder, sifted

FILLING

12 ounces (340 g) dark chocolate, chopped

¾ cup (177 ml) heavy whipping cream

2 tablespoons salted butter

TOPPING

Coarse sea salt

Preheat the oven to 350°F.

TO MAKE THE CRUST: Add the graham crackers, butter, cane sugar, and cocoa to a food processor. Process until completely combined, there are no pieces of graham cracker, and the crust looks uniform.

Using your hands, form into a 9½-inch tart pan by pushing the crust onto the sides first and then pressing the remaining crust into the bottom.

Bake for 5 to 7 minutes, until dry and set.

TO MAKE THE FILLING: Using a double boiler, add the chocolate and melt completely. Slowly add the cream and stir to combine until all the cream has been added. Remove from the heat, add the butter, and stir to combine completely. Pour the filling into the crust and allow to set completely, about 4 hours.

Sprinkle the top with coarse sea salt.

Store in the fridge for up to 5 days.

GLUTEN-FREE

Use gluten-free graham crackers, make sure to weigh them to 204 grams, as gluten-free graham crackers usually come in different sizes.

HIGH ALTITUDE

Follow the recipe as noted.

RASPBERRY RHUBARB TART

MAKES A 9½-INCH TART

The perfect ending to a backyard barbecue. This buttery and flaky crust complements the sweet and tart mixture of rhubarb and raspberry. A little hint of cardamom adds allure, and an almond whipped cream topping seals the deal. This dessert is summer in a tart pan.

CRUST

¾ cup (95 g) all-purpose flour

½ teaspoon cane sugar

6 tablespoons (85 g) salted butter, cold

3 tablespoons (45 ml) cold water

FILLING

1 cup (2 to 3 stalks) chopped rhubarb

½ cup (113 g) cane sugar

6 ounces (170 g) raspberries

3 tablespoons (21 g) all-purpose flour

1 teaspoon cornstarch

¼ teaspoon cardamom

TOPPING

1 cup (237 ml) heavy whipping cream

½ cup (71 g) powdered sugar, sifted

½ teaspoon almond extract

HIGH ALTITUDE

Bake at 350°F for 20 minutes for the first parbake, remove the pie weights and parchment paper, and bake again for 10 minutes. Once filled, bake for 15 to 20 minutes, until set.

TO MAKE THE CRUST: In the bowl of a stand mixer fitted with the paddle attachment, add the flour and cane sugar. Turn on low for two to three rotations to combine the dry ingredients.

Remove the butter from the fridge and cut the stick into four pieces. From there, chop the pieces into small cubes; the smaller the cubes, the flakier the crust. Add the cold cubed butter to the flour mixture. Measure out the cold water and have it ready.

Turn the mixer on low and slowly start to incorporate all the flour, cane sugar, and butter. Gradually turn the mixer to medium speed. Once the butter mixture looks like wet sand, immediately add in all the cold water. As soon as the dough comes together, stop the mixer.

Form the dough into a disk and wrap in plastic wrap. Allow to cool in the fridge for at least 6 hours or overnight.

Preheat the oven to 350°F. On a floured surface, roll out the crust to ¼ inch thick. Place in a 9½-inch tart pan and form against the sides. Fold over any edges to create even sides that are flush with the edge of the pan.

Place a piece of parchment paper into the tart pan and fill with rice or pie weights. Parbake the crust for 25 minutes, remove the pie weights and parchment paper, and bake again for 15 minutes.

TO MAKE THE FILLING: In a small saucepan, add the rhubarb and cane sugar. Cook over low heat and allow the sugar to dissolve, stirring occasionally. Once the sugar melts, continue to simmer on low until the sugar has reduced and the mixture is thick, about 10 to 15 minutes. Remove from heat.

Add the raspberries, flour, cornstarch, and cardamom to the rhubarb mixture and stir to combine completely. Pour into the tart crust and spread evenly. Bake for 20 to 25 minutes, until set. Allow to cool completely.

TO MAKE THE TOPPING: In the bowl of a stand mixer fitted with the whisk attachment, add the whipping cream, powdered sugar, and

almond extract. Mix on low and gradually increase the speed as the mixture thickens; whisk until stiff peaks form.

Top the tart with the cream topping and spread evenly.

Store in the fridge for up to 3 days.

LEMON BLUEBERRY TART

MAKES A 9½-INCH TART

Lemon and blueberry is one of my favorite combinations—the blueberries bursting with flavor are complemented so well by the sweet and tart lemon. This tart can double for breakfast or dessert, which I completely adore.

CRUST

¾ cup (95 g) all-purpose flour

½ teaspoon cane sugar

6 tablespoons (85 g) salted butter, cold

3 tablespoons (45 ml) cold water

FILLING

½ cup (113 g) cane sugar

Zest of 1 lemon

1½ teaspoons cornstarch

3 tablespoons (21 g) all-purpose flour

Pinch of fine sea salt

15 ounces (425 g) blueberries

TOPPING

1 cup (127 g) all-purpose flour

½ cup (113 g) packed light brown sugar

6 tablespoons (85 g) salted butter, melted

GLAZE

½ cup (71 g) powdered sugar, sifted

1 tablespoon (15 ml) lemon juice

HIGH ALTITUDE

Bake at 350°F for 20 minutes for the first parbake, remove the pie weights and parchment paper, and bake again for 10 minutes. Once filled, bake for 20 to 25 minutes, until golden brown.

TO MAKE THE CRUST: In the bowl of a stand mixer fitted with the paddle attachment, add the flour and cane sugar. Turn on low for two to three rotations to combine the dry ingredients.

Remove the butter from the fridge and cut the stick into four pieces. From there, chop the pieces into small cubes; the smaller the cubes, the flakier the crust. Add the cold cubed butter to the flour mixture. Measure out the cold water and have it ready.

Turn the mixer on low and slowly start to incorporate all the flour, cane sugar, and butter. Gradually turn the mixer to medium speed. Once the butter mixture looks like wet sand, immediately add in all the water. As soon as the dough comes together, stop the mixer.

Form the dough into a disk and wrap in plastic wrap. Allow to cool in the fridge for at least 6 hours or overnight.

Preheat the oven to 350°F.

On a floured surface, roll out the crust to ¼ inch thick. Place in a 9½-inch tart pan and form against the sides. Fold over any edges to create even sides that are flush with the edge of the pan.

Place a piece of parchment paper into the tart pan and fill with rice or pie weights. Parbake the crust for 25 minutes, remove the pie weights and parchment paper, and bake again for 15 minutes.

TO MAKE THE FILLING: In a medium bowl, add the cane sugar, lemon zest, cornstarch, flour, and sea salt and whisk together. Add the blueberries and stir together until you don't see any dry bits and the blueberries are completely coated. Set aside.

TO MAKE THE TOPPING: In a medium bowl, add the flour, brown sugar, and melted butter. Stir with a spatula until combined.

Fill the tart crust with the blueberry filling and top with the crumble.

Bake for 25 to 30 minutes, until golden brown. Allow to cool completely.

TO MAKE THE GLAZE: In a medium bowl, add the powdered sugar and lemon juice and whisk together until you have a smooth glaze. Drizzle over the top of the tart.

Store in a cool dry place for up to 3 days.

RASPBERRY PEACH PIE

MAKES A 9-INCH PIE

During the summer, both raspberries and peaches are in season, which means they are at their most flavorful. Fresh peaches bring sweetness to this pie, while the raspberries bring a tart flavor that balances the fruity sweetness and buttery crust. This pie is obviously an egg-free delight, but another perk is its lower sugar content—letting the fruit shine!

CRUST

2 cups (255 g) all-purpose flour

½ teaspoon cane sugar

¾ cup (170 g) salted butter, cold

½ cup (118 ml) cold water

Pie Wash (page 163)

FILLING

½ cup (113 g) cane sugar

3 tablespoons (21 g) all-purpose flour

1 teaspoon cornstarch

¼ teaspoon fine sea salt

2 large peaches, pitted and sliced

6 ounces (170 g) raspberries

HIGH ALTITUDE

Bake at 350°F for 1 hour, or until golden brown.

TO MAKE THE CRUST: In the bowl of a stand mixer fitted with the paddle attachment, add the flour and cane sugar. Turn on low for two to three rotations to combine the dry ingredients.

Remove the butter from the fridge, cut the stick into four pieces, and then chop into small cubes from there. The smaller the cubes, the flakier the crust. Add the cold cubed butter to the flour mixture. Measure out the cold water and have it ready.

Turn the mixer on low and slowly start to incorporate the ingredients. Gradually turn the mixer to medium speed. Once the butter mixture looks like wet sand, immediately add in all the cold water. As soon as the dough comes together, stop the mixer.

Have two pieces of plastic wrap ready and divide the dough into a top and bottom. The bottom should weigh about 11 ounces (312 g) and the top 6 ounces (170 g). Form each piece into a disk and wrap in plastic wrap. Allow to cool in the fridge overnight.

Preheat the oven to 350°F. Have the pie wash ready.

TO MAKE THE FILLING: In a medium bowl, add the cane sugar, flour, cornstarch, and sea salt and whisk together. Add the peaches and raspberries and fold with a spatula to coat completely. Set aside.

Remove the pie dough from the fridge. Remove the plastic wrap and place the dough on a floured surface. First, roll out the large disk to ¼ inch thick; it should be about 11 inches in diameter. Place the pie dough into the pie pan and press lightly to form against the pan. It should be large enough that the dough folds right over the top. Roll out the smaller disk to ¼ inch thick; it should be about 9 inches in diameter. Set aside.

Add the filling into the pie pan and spread evenly.

Gently place the top pie dough on top. Crimp the two together, then roll the excess dough into the pie pan so it's even with the edges of the pan and creates an edge that seals the filling in. Flute the edges by using the thumb and index finger of your right hand to pinch the rolled edge of dough and pushing the index finger of your left hand into it to create the "flute." Continue around the entire pie crust.

Using a pastry brush, brush the dough with the pie wash. Make four vents in the top of the pie with a sharp knife.

Bake for 1 hour 15 minutes, or until golden brown.

Store at room temperature for up to 3 days.

PECAN PIE

MAKES A 9-INCH PIE

Pecan pie is a classic dessert for Thanksgiving and Christmas. When I was growing up, it was something we always had during these holidays. I have vivid memories of sneaking bites of the pecan pie filling right out of the pie. My mom would always scold me for just wanting the sugary insides! The filling was always my favorite part. While I have grown to appreciate the whole pie now, the filling is truly the star. Although a pecan pie filling usually contains eggs, this egg-free version will still take you down memory lane.

CRUST

1 cup (127 g) all-purpose flour

½ teaspoon cane sugar

½ cup (113 g) salted butter, cold

¼ cup (59 ml) cold water

Pie Wash (page 163)

FILLING

½ cup (113 g) packed dark brown sugar

¼ cup (78 g) light corn syrup

¼ cup (57 g) salted butter

1 tablespoon (22 g) maple syrup

1 teaspoon aquafaba powder

⅓ cup (78 ml) water

3 tablespoons (21 g) all-purpose flour

3 tablespoons (21 g) cornstarch

1½ teaspoons cinnamon

¼ teaspoon fine sea salt

1⅓ cups (170 g) pecans

HIGH ALTITUDE

Parbake at 350°F for 15 minutes. Once filled, bake for 25 to 30 minutes, until the crust is golden brown and the filling is bubbly.

TO MAKE THE CRUST: In the bowl of a stand mixer fitted with the paddle attachment, add the flour and cane sugar. Turn on low for two to three rotations to combine the dry ingredients.

Remove the butter from the fridge, cut the stick into four pieces, and then chop into small cubes from there. The smaller the cubes, the flakier the crust. Add the cold cubed butter to the flour mixture. Measure out the cold water and have it ready.

Turn the mixer on low and slowly start to incorporate the ingredients. Gradually turn the mixer to medium speed. Once the butter mixture looks like wet sand, immediately add in all the cold water. As soon as the dough comes together, stop the mixer.

Have a piece of plastic wrap ready. Form the dough into a disk and wrap in plastic wrap. Allow to cool in the fridge overnight.

Preheat the oven to 350°F.

Remove the pie dough from the fridge. Remove the plastic wrap and place the dough on a floured surface. Roll out the dough into a disk that is ¼ inch thick; it should be about 11 inches in diameter. Place the pie dough into the pie pan and press lightly to form against the pan. It should be large enough that the dough folds right over the top of the pan.

Roll the excess dough into the pie pan so it's even with the edges of the pan. Flute the edges by using the thumb and index finger of your right hand to pinch the rolled edge of dough and pushing the index finger of your left hand into it to create the "flute." Continue around the entire pie crust.

Place a piece of parchment paper into the pie pan and form it to the sides. Add rice or pie weights and parbake for 20 minutes. Remove the parchment paper and weights. Using a pastry brush, brush the fluted crust with the pie wash.

TO MAKE THE FILLING: In a small saucepan, add the brown sugar, corn syrup, butter, and maple syrup and cook over medium heat until the butter is melted and completely combined. Allow to cook for 2 to 3 more minutes, until it starts to bubble; remove from heat.

In a small bowl, add the aquafaba and water; stir to combine completely.

Add the flour, cornstarch, cinnamon, sea salt, and aquafaba mixture into the brown sugar mixture and whisk to combine completely. Next, add the pecans and stir to combine completely.

Transfer to the crust and bake for 30 to 35 minutes, until the crust is golden brown and the filling is bubbly. It will not be set when you remove it from the oven. Allow to cool completely; the pie will set as it cools.

Store in a cool dry place for up to 3 days.

TRIPLE BERRY PIE

MAKES A 9-INCH PIE

This pie uses strawberries, blackberries, and raspberries. But you can easily switch it up and use any type of berries you have, as long as the total volume is still the same! This easy swap makes this recipe super adaptable. You'll want to make it again and again, so try out different flavor combinations.

CRUST

2 cups (255 g) all-purpose flour

½ teaspoon cane sugar

¾ cup (170 g) salted butter, cold

½ cup (118 ml) cold water

Pie Wash (page 163)

FILLING

½ cup (113 g) cane sugar

3 tablespoons (21 g) all-purpose flour

1 teaspoon cornstarch

¼ teaspoon fine sea salt

6 ounces (170 g) blackberries

6 ounces (170 g) raspberries

6 ounces (170 g) strawberries, de-stemmed and sliced

HIGH ALTITUDE

Bake at 350°F for 1 hour, or until golden brown.

TO MAKE THE CRUST: In the bowl of a stand mixer fitted with the paddle attachment, add the flour and cane sugar. Turn on low for two to three rotations to combine the dry ingredients.

Remove the butter from the fridge, cut the stick into four pieces, and then chop into small cubes from there. The smaller the cubes, the flakier the crust. Add the cold cubed butter to the flour mixture. Measure out the cold water and have it ready.

Turn the mixer on low and slowly start to incorporate the ingredients. Gradually turn the mixer to medium speed. Once the butter mixture looks like wet sand, immediately add in all the cold water. As soon as the dough comes together, stop the mixer.

Have two pieces of plastic wrap ready, and divide the dough into a top and bottom. The bottom should weigh about 11 ounces (312 g) and the top 6 ounces (170 g). Form each piece into a disk and wrap in plastic wrap. Allow to cool in the fridge overnight.

Preheat the oven to 350°F. Have the pie wash ready.

TO MAKE THE FILLING: In a medium bowl, add the cane sugar, flour, cornstarch, and sea salt and whisk together. Add the blackberries, raspberries, and strawberries and fold with a spatula to coat completely. Set aside.

Remove the pie dough from the fridge. Remove the plastic wrap and place the dough on a floured surface. First, roll out the large disk to ¼ inch thick; it should be about 11 inches in diameter. Place the pie dough into the pie pan and press lightly to form against the pan. It should be large enough that the dough folds right over the top. Roll out the smaller disk to ¼ inch thick; it should be about 9 inches in diameter. Set aside.

Add the filling into the pie pan and spread evenly.

I like to use a pizza cutter for this next step, but a sharp knife will work as well. Cut the rolled-out dough into 1-inch-wide strips. Place the strips on top of the filling horizontally, leaving 1 inch between

the strips. Use the smaller strips toward the sides of the pie and the longer strips for the middle. Next, add the remaining dough strips vertically, alternating each strip over and under the horizontal ones.

Once the lattice top is complete, roll the excess dough into the pie pan so it's even with the edges of the pan. Flute the edges by using the thumb and index finger of your right hand to pinch the rolled edge of dough and pushing the index finger of your left hand into it to create the "flute." Continue around the entire pie crust. Using a pastry brush, brush the dough with the pie wash.

Bake for 1 hour 15 minutes, or until golden brown.

Store at room temperature for up to 3 days.

Cakes

When you need a little something more than a loaf cake or something to serve a crowd, then I suggest you bake a layer cake, a sheet cake, cupcakes, or cake balls. While cake balls are probably my absolute favorite, all of these cakes are sure to impress.

For eggless cakes, I prefer to use real ingredients that you'd normally have in your fridge. I love using heavy whipping cream, as the velvety texture brings moisture as well as fat to cake, which is crucial for a delicate crumb that isn't dry. I also use applesauce as a binder and to help create a fluffy texture that mimics eggs.

If you are just learning to bake cakes, start out with my easy sheet cakes first. If you need a larger cake, simply double any of the 6-inch cake recipes and bake them in 9-inch cake pans. If you do, just be sure to add baking time, about 3 to 6 minutes, and always test with a toothpick to make sure they are done.

It's super important to store cakes in an airtight container so they don't dry out after they've been cut. I highly recommend a cake dome for this! A cake dome is also a great place to store a cake if you want to make it the day before a dinner party or a celebration.

CHOCOLATE WHIPPED CREAM CAKE

MAKES A TWO-LAYER 6-INCH CAKE

Light and fluffy whipped cream frosting paired with chocolate cake and fresh berries—there really is no other quintessential cake. If you're looking for a different but equally delicious cake, you can switch up the fruit or use strawberries alone. Regardless of your preferred fruity flavors, the texture of this cake is moist and fluffy, which pairs perfectly with the whipped cream frosting.

BATTER

½ cup (113 g) salted butter, softened

¾ cup (170 g) cane sugar

1 teaspoon vanilla extract

½ cup (118 ml) milk, room temperature

½ cup (113 g) sour cream, room temperature

¼ cup (57 g) applesauce, room temperature

¼ cup (59 ml) heavy whipping cream, room temperature

1 cup (142 g) cake flour

⅔ cup (57 g) Dutch cocoa powder, sifted

¾ teaspoon baking powder

½ teaspoon fine sea salt

FROSTING

1 cup (237 ml) heavy whipping cream

½ cup (71 g) powdered sugar, sifted

½ teaspoon vanilla extract

TOPPING

6 ounces (170 g) blackberries

6 ounces (170 g) blueberries

6 ounces (170 g) raspberries

Preheat the oven to 350°F. Line two 6-inch cake pans with parchment paper and lightly grease and flour the sides.

TO MAKE THE BATTER: In the bowl of a stand mixer fitted with the paddle attachment, add the butter, cane sugar, and vanilla extract. Mix on low until combined and there are no chunks of butter.

Add the milk, sour cream, applesauce, and whipping cream and mix to combine.

In a separate bowl, add the cake flour, cocoa, baking powder, and sea salt and whisk together. With the mixer on low, slowly add in the cake flour mixture and mix until a smooth batter forms.

Divide the batter evenly into each cake pan, about 14 ounces (397 g) each.

Bake for 30 to 34 minutes, until a toothpick inserted in the center comes out clean. Allow to cool completely in the cake pans.

TO MAKE THE FROSTING: In the bowl of a stand mixer fitted with the whisk attachment, add the whipping cream, powdered sugar, and vanilla extract. Whisk, starting on low to avoid splattering, then gradually increase the speed as the mixture starts to thicken. Whisk until peaks form and the frosting is light and fluffy.

On a cake stand or spinner, add the first cake layer. Add half the frosting and spread evenly, then top with half the berries. Top with the second cake layer, spread the remaining frosting on top, and top with the rest of the berries.

Store in the fridge for up to 3 days.

GLUTEN-FREE

Replace the cake flour with ¾ cup plus 2 tablespoons (142 g) gluten-free flour blend.

HIGH ALTITUDE

Bake at 350°F for 25 to 28 minutes, until a toothpick inserted in the center comes out clean.

PUMPKIN SPICE CARROT CAKE

MAKES A THREE-LAYER 6-INCH CAKE

Fruits and vegetables are a great way to add moisture and structure to desserts without eggs. And carrot cake holds a special place in my heart, as it was the first cake recipe I developed on my own. This is an eggless variation of my classic carrot cake. But . . . I've added pumpkin and spice for a fall-inspired twist and replaced the nutmeg that is in traditional pumpkin spice with cardamom. You'll be making this cake again and again!

BATTER

½ cup (118 ml) canola oil

1 cup (226 g) cane sugar

5 ounces (142 g) carrots, finely grated

½ cup (118 ml) milk

¼ cup (62 g) pumpkin puree

1¼ cups (177 g) cake flour

1½ teaspoons cinnamon

1 teaspoon ginger

1 teaspoon cloves

1 teaspoon baking powder

¾ teaspoon fine sea salt

½ teaspoon cardamom

FROSTING

3 cups (425 g) powdered sugar, sifted

½ cup (113 g) salted butter, softened

½ cup (113 g) cream cheese

1 teaspoon vanilla extract

TOPPING

Cinnamon sticks (optional)

Preheat the oven to 350°F. Line three 6-inch cake pans with parchment paper and lightly grease and flour the sides.

TO MAKE THE BATTER: In the bowl of a stand mixer fitted with the paddle attachment, add the canola oil, cane sugar, carrots, milk, and pumpkin and mix on low until combined.

In a separate bowl, add the cake flour, cinnamon, ginger, cloves, baking powder, sea salt, and cardamom and whisk together. Add to the sugar mixture and mix on low until a batter forms, scraping down the sides of the bowl as needed. Divide the batter evenly into each cake pan, about 9.5 ounces (269 g) each.

Bake for 20 to 24 minutes, until a toothpick inserted in the center comes out clean. Allow to cool completely in the cake pans.

TO MAKE THE FROSTING: In the bowl of a stand mixer, add the powdered sugar, butter, cream cheese, and vanilla extract. Mix on low until combined, then speed up the mixer to high for 1 minute, or until light and fluffy.

Transfer the frosting to a piping bag with Ateco tip #827. Place the first cake layer on a cake stand or spinner. Pipe the frosting around the outer edge of the cake and spiral into the middle. Repeat with each layer. Top with cinnamon sticks, if using.

Store in an airtight container in the fridge for up to 3 days.

GLUTEN-FREE

Replace the cake flour with 1 cup plus 2 tablespoons (177 g) gluten-free flour blend.

HIGH ALTITUDE

Bake at 350°F for 18 to 22 minutes, until a toothpick inserted in the center comes out clean.

BIRTHDAY SHEET CAKE

MAKES A 9-BY-13-INCH SHEET CAKE

This is my baked-from-scratch version of every single birthday cake I had growing up. My mom would bake all our birthday cakes, and each year she'd ask if we wanted chocolate or vanilla—that was it; we weren't given any other options because she wasn't really a baker. She used a box of cake mix, but she made her own icing from scratch. And she baked it in a 9-by-13-inch glass dish. There is a big difference between frosting and icing, as far as I'm concerned. Icing is extra sweet, not as thick, and has a creamy texture compared to frosting. This icing is exactly like my mom used to make!

BATTER

1 cup (226 g) salted butter, softened

1½ cups (340 g) cane sugar

1 cup (237 ml) chocolate milk, room temperature

½ cup (113 g) applesauce, room temperature

½ cup (113 g) sour cream, room temperature

2 cups (284 g) cake flour

⅔ cup (57 g) Dutch cocoa powder, sifted

1½ teaspoons baking powder

1 teaspoon fine sea salt

1 teaspoon ground vanilla bean

ICING

Heaping 2⅓ cups (340 g) powdered sugar, sifted

½ cup (118 ml) heavy whipping cream

¼ cup (57 g) salted butter, softened

1 teaspoon vanilla extract

TOPPING

Rainbow sprinkles (optional)

Preheat the oven to 350°F. Line a 9-by-13-inch baking pan with parchment paper.

TO MAKE THE BATTER: In the bowl of a stand mixer fitted with the paddle attachment, add the butter and cane sugar and mix on low until combined and there are no chunks of butter.

Add the chocolate milk, applesauce, and sour cream and mix on low to combine.

Add the cake flour, cocoa, baking powder, sea salt, and ground vanilla bean in that order and mix on low to combine into a smooth batter, scraping down the sides of the bowl as needed. Transfer to the prepared baking pan and spread evenly.

Bake for 30 to 35 minutes, until a toothpick inserted in the center comes out clean. Allow to cool completely in the pan.

TO MAKE THE ICING: In the bowl of a stand mixer fitted with the paddle attachment, add the powdered sugar, whipping cream, butter, and vanilla extract and mix on low until combined. Speed up the mixer to high and mix for 1 to 2 minutes, until light and fluffy.

Spread the icing over the top of the cake and top with rainbow sprinkles, if using.

Store in an airtight container in the fridge for up to 3 days.

GLUTEN-FREE

Replace the cake flour with 1¾ cups (269 g) gluten-free flour blend.

HIGH ALTITUDE

Bake at 350°F for 25 to 30 minutes, until a toothpick inserted in the center comes out clean.

STRAWBERRY WHIPPED CREAM SHEET CAKE

MAKES A 9-BY-13-INCH SHEET CAKE

Summertime wouldn't be complete without a strawberry whipped cream cake. Similar to strawberry shortcake, this easy sheet cake is topped with my favorite whipped cream frosting and fresh strawberries. This cake reminds me of one my mom made for backyard barbecues. It was a favorite of ours, and I hope it becomes a favorite in your home as well.

BATTER

Scant 5 cups (680 g) cake flour

2 cups (454 g) cane sugar

2 teaspoons baking powder

1 teaspoon fine sea salt

1 cup (226 g) applesauce

1 cup (237 ml) canola oil

½ cup (118 ml) heavy whipping cream

½ cup (118 ml) milk

FROSTING

2 cups (473 ml) heavy whipping cream

1 cup (142 g) powdered sugar, sifted

1 teaspoon vanilla extract

TOPPING

6 ounces (170 g) strawberries, sliced

Preheat the oven to 350°F. Line a 9-by-13-inch baking pan with parchment paper.

TO MAKE THE BATTER: In the bowl of a stand mixer fitted with the paddle attachment, add the cake flour, cane sugar, baking powder, and sea salt and mix on low for two to three rotations to combine the dry ingredients.

Add the applesauce, canola oil, whipping cream, and milk and mix on low until combined into a smooth batter. Transfer to the prepared baking pan.

Bake for 40 to 45 minutes, until a toothpick inserted in the center comes out clean. Allow to cool completely in the pan.

TO MAKE THE FROSTING: In the bowl of a stand mixer fitted with the whisk attachment, add the whipping cream, powdered sugar, and vanilla extract. Mix, starting on low to avoid splattering, then gradually increase the speed until you are at full speed. Mix until light and fluffy and it doesn't fall off the whisk.

Spread the frosting over the top of the cake and top with the strawberries.

Store in the fridge for up to 3 days.

GLUTEN-FREE

Replace the cake flour with a scant 1½ cups (226 g) gluten-free flour blend and 1¾ cups (170 g) coconut flour.

HIGH ALTITUDE

Bake at 350°F for 35 to 40 minutes, until a toothpick inserted in the center comes out clean.

LEMON GINGER SHEET CAKE

MAKES A 9-BY-13-INCH SHEET CAKE

As someone who is completely and utterly in love with chocolate, sometimes it's difficult for me to even fathom desserts without it, cake included. But my younger brother is one of those people who doesn't care for chocolate. All through our childhood, I always found my way to other desserts through his preferences as we were compromising and sharing. Every time we enjoyed a lemon dessert, or an orange dessert, or a vanilla dessert, I was thankful he had talked me into it. Even before I became a baker, I always wanted to bake for others—and this is a cake I've baked often for those who have preferences aside from chocolate! The combination of the sweet lemon and the subtle spice of the ginger is what takes this beyond just another lemon cake.

BATTER

1 cup (226 g) salted butter, softened

1½ cups (340 g) cane sugar

1 cup (237 ml) milk, room temperature

½ cup (113 g) sour cream, room temperature

¼ cup (57 g) applesauce, room temperature

2 cups (284 g) cake flour

1½ teaspoons baking powder

1 teaspoon ginger

1 teaspoon fine sea salt

FROSTING

3 cups plus 3 tablespoons (454 g) powdered sugar, sifted

1 cup (226 g) salted butter, softened

1 tablespoon fresh lemon juice

2 teaspoons lemon flavor

Zest of 1 lemon for topping

Preheat the oven to 350°F. Line a 9-by-13-inch baking pan with parchment paper.

TO MAKE THE BATTER: In the bowl of a stand mixer fitted with the paddle attachment, add the butter and cane sugar and mix on low until combined and there are no chunks of butter.

Add the milk, sour cream, and applesauce and mix on low to combine.

Add the cake flour, baking powder, ginger, and sea salt in that order and mix on low to combine into a smooth batter, scraping down the sides of the bowl as needed. Transfer to the prepared baking pan and spread evenly.

Bake for 30 to 35 minutes, until a toothpick inserted in the center comes out clean.

TO MAKE THE FROSTING: In the bowl of a stand mixer fitted with the paddle attachment, add the powdered sugar, butter, lemon juice, and lemon flavor and mix on low until combined. Speed up the mixer to high and mix for 1 to 2 minutes, until light and fluffy.

Once the cake has cooled, spread the frosting over the top of the cake and top with lemon zest.

Store in an airtight container in the fridge for up to 3 days.

GLUTEN-FREE

Replace the cake flour with 1¾ cups (269 g) gluten-free flour blend.

HIGH ALTITUDE

Bake at 350°F for 25 to 30 minutes, until a toothpick inserted in the center comes out clean.

PEANUT BUTTER & JELLY SHEET CAKE

MAKES A 9-BY-13-INCH SHEET CAKE

When I was little, I was not a fan of jelly. I'm not sure how my mom even allowed this to happen or what sparked my dislike as a child. So I always just had plain peanut butter sandwiches. When I finally came to my senses, I think I ate peanut butter and jellies for a straight week. I mean, c'mon, it's a classic combination for a reason! This cake brings a sweetness from the raspberry jam that complements that creamy and salty peanut butter flavor just perfectly. Switch it up with any jam flavor you like best!

BATTER

1 cup (226 g) salted butter, softened

1½ cups (340 g) cane sugar

1 teaspoon vanilla extract

1 cup (237 ml) milk, room temperature

½ cup (113 g) applesauce, room temperature

⅓ cup (71 g) peanut butter

2 cups (284 g) cake flour

1 teaspoon baking powder

1 teaspoon fine sea salt

FROSTING

3 cups (425 g) powdered sugar, sifted

1 cup (226 g) salted butter, softened

⅓ cup (71 g) peanut butter

2 tablespoons milk

TOPPINGS

6 ounces (170 g) raspberry jam

6 ounces (170 g) raspberries

Preheat the oven to 350°F. Line a 9-by-13-inch baking pan with parchment paper.

TO MAKE THE BATTER: In the bowl of a stand mixer fitted with the paddle attachment, add the butter, cane sugar, and vanilla extract and mix on low until combined and there are no chunks of butter.

Add the milk, applesauce, and peanut butter and mix on low until combined.

Add the cake flour, baking powder, and sea salt in that order. Mix on low until a smooth batter forms. Transfer to the prepared baking pan.

Bake for 30 to 35 minutes, until a toothpick inserted in the center comes out clean. Allow to cool completely in the pan.

TO MAKE THE FROSTING: In the bowl of a stand mixer fitted with the paddle attachment, add the powdered sugar, butter, peanut butter, and milk. Mix on low until combined, then speed up the mixer to high for 1 minute or until light and fluffy.

Spread the raspberry jam over the top of the cake. Place in the fridge for 15 to 20 minutes to cool the jam; this makes it easier to spread the frosting on top. Remove from the fridge and top with the frosting, spreading it evenly. Top with raspberries.

Store in the fridge for up to 3 days.

GLUTEN-FREE

Replace the cake flour with 1¾ cups (269 g) gluten-free flour blend.

HIGH ALTITUDE

Bake at 350°F for 25 to 30 minutes, until a toothpick inserted in the center comes out clean.

VANILLA CUPCAKES

MAKES 15 CUPCAKES

Sometimes simple and delicious is all you need. Birthdays, Fourth of July, Christmas, New Year's, Easter . . . there isn't a celebration when these cupcakes wouldn't be appropriate. I use a combination of heavy whipping cream and applesauce to make these cupcakes light and fluffy. This combination also provides a slightly sweet but neutral flavor so the vanilla can shine through.

BATTER

Heaping 2⅓ cups (340 g) cake flour

1 cup (226 g) cane sugar

1 teaspoon baking powder

½ teaspoon fine sea salt

½ cup (118 ml) canola oil

½ cup (118 ml) heavy whipping cream

½ cup (113 g) applesauce

¼ cup (57 g) sour cream

1 teaspoon vanilla extract

FROSTING

3 cups plus 3 tablespoons (454 g) powdered sugar, sifted

1 cup (226 g) salted butter

1 to 2 teaspoons milk

1 teaspoon vanilla extract

TOPPING

Rainbow sprinkles (optional)

Preheat the oven to 350°F. Line two cupcake pans with liners.

TO MAKE THE BATTER: In the bowl of a stand mixer fitted with the paddle attachment, add the cake flour, cane sugar, baking powder, and sea salt and mix on low for two to three rotations to combine the dry ingredients.

Add the canola oil, whipping cream, applesauce, sour cream, and vanilla extract and mix on low until combined into a smooth batter.

Scoop the batter into the prepared pans, filling three-quarters full.

Bake for 20 to 24 minutes, until a toothpick inserted in the center comes out clean. Allow to cool completely in the pans.

TO MAKE THE FROSTING: In the bowl of a stand mixer fitted with the paddle attachment, add the powdered sugar, butter, milk, and vanilla extract. Mix on low until combined and then speed up the mixer to high for 1 minute, or until light and fluffy.

Frost the cupcakes with a piping bag or spatula. Dip, roll, or sprinkle with rainbow sprinkles, if using.

Store in an airtight container for up to 3 days.

GLUTEN-FREE

Replace the cake flour with ¾ cup (113 g) gluten-free flour blend and ¾ cup plus 2 tablespoons (85 g) coconut flour.

HIGH ALTITUDE

Bake at 350°F for 18 to 22 minutes, until a toothpick inserted in the center comes out clean.

HONEY BANANA CUPCAKES

MAKES 12 CUPCAKES

I love using bananas in desserts, as they provide moisture, structure, and fluffiness like no other! These banana cupcakes are topped with a honey buttercream for a light and simple cupcake. There are many different kinds of honey. Switch it up and you'll get a slightly different flavor each time. Try an orange blossom honey, which is one of my faves!

BATTER

½ cup (113 g) salted butter, softened

¾ cup (170 g) cane sugar

1 teaspoon vanilla extract

2 large ripe bananas

½ cup (118 ml) milk, room temperature

¼ cup (59 ml) heavy whipping cream, room temperature

¼ cup (57 g) sour cream, room temperature

1 cup plus 3 tablespoons (170 g) cake flour

¾ teaspoon baking powder

½ teaspoon fine sea salt

FROSTING

3 cups plus 3 tablespoons (454 g) powdered sugar, sifted

1 cup (226 g) salted butter, softened

2 tablespoons (43 g) raw honey

1 teaspoon vanilla extract

Preheat the oven to 350°F. Line a cupcake pan with liners.

TO MAKE THE BATTER: In the bowl of a stand mixer fitted with the paddle attachment, add the butter, cane sugar, and vanilla extract. Mix on low until combined and there are no chunks of butter.

Add the bananas, milk, whipping cream, and sour cream and mix to combine.

In a separate bowl, add the cake flour, baking powder, and sea salt and whisk together. With the mixer on low, slowly add in the cake flour mixture and mix until a smooth batter forms. Scoop the batter into the prepared pan, filling three-quarters full.

Bake for 20 to 24 minutes, until a toothpick inserted in the center comes out clean. Allow to cool completely in the pans.

TO MAKE THE FROSTING: In the bowl of a stand mixer fitted with the paddle attachment, add the powdered sugar, butter, honey, and vanilla extract. Mix on low until combined and then speed up the mixer to high for 1 minute, or until light and fluffy. Transfer to a piping bag with Ateco tip #846.

Pipe the frosting on top of each cupcake.

Store in an airtight container for up to 3 days.

GLUTEN-FREE

Replace the cake flour with 1 cup plus 1 tablespoon plus 1 teaspoon (170 g) gluten-free flour blend.

HIGH ALTITUDE

Bake at 350°F for 18 to 22 minutes, until a toothpick inserted in the center comes out clean.

DARK CHOCOLATE ESPRESSO CUPCAKES

MAKES 16 CUPCAKES

It's the little things in life that make me happy, and these cupcakes are one of them. I love the flavor of coffee but I don't drink it, so it's such a treat to make these cupcakes. When baking I like to use espresso powder, as it can give an amazing espresso flavor without adding the extra liquid of an actual espresso shot.

BATTER

2 cups (284 g) cake flour

1 cup (226 g) cane sugar

½ cup (43 g) Dutch cocoa powder, sifted

2 teaspoons espresso powder

1 teaspoon baking powder

½ teaspoon fine sea salt

½ cup (118 ml) canola oil

½ cup (118 ml) chocolate milk

½ cup (113 g) applesauce

½ cup (113 g) sour cream

1 teaspoon vanilla extract

FROSTING

3 cups (425 g) powdered sugar, sifted

1 cup (226 g) salted butter, softened

2 teaspoons espresso powder

1 to 2 teaspoons milk

TOPPING

3 ounces dark chocolate, broken into pieces

Preheat the oven to 350°F. Line two cupcake pans with liners.

TO MAKE THE BATTER: In the bowl of a stand mixer fitted with the paddle attachment, add the cake flour, cane sugar, cocoa, espresso powder, baking powder, and sea salt and mix on low for two to three rotations to combine the dry ingredients.

Add the canola oil, chocolate milk, applesauce, sour cream, and vanilla extract and mix on low until combined into a smooth batter.

Scoop the batter into the prepared pans, filling three-quarters full.

Bake for 20 to 24 minutes, until a toothpick inserted in the center comes out clean. Allow to cool completely in the pans.

TO MAKE THE FROSTING: In the bowl of a stand mixer fitted with the paddle attachment, add the powdered sugar, butter, espresso powder, and milk. Mix on low until combined and then speed up the mixer to high for 1 minute, or until light and fluffy.

Transfer the frosting to a piping bag with Ateco tip #808 or no tip. Frost the cupcakes by piping a large dollop onto each one.

Stick a piece of dark chocolate on top.

Store in an airtight container for up to 3 days.

GLUTEN-FREE

Replace the cake flour with ¾ cup (71 g) coconut flour and ¼ cup plus 2½ tablespoons (57 g) gluten-free flour blend.

HIGH ALTITUDE

Bake at 350°F for 18 to 22 minutes, until a toothpick inserted in the center comes out clean.

LEMON CUPCAKES WITH CREAM CHEESE FROSTING

MAKES 12 CUPCAKES

Sweet, tart, and tangy—these cupcakes are a dream. Canola oil helps bake up a moist and tender cake, and I like to use it with cakes that have lighter flavors, such as this lemon cupcake. I use applesauce and heavy cream in place of eggs, as they complement this flavor and make a light and delicate cake batter. Make sure to store these cupcakes in the fridge, as the cream cheese frosting needs to be refrigerated.

BATTER

Heaping 2⅓ cups (340 g) cake flour

1 cup (226 g) cane sugar

1 teaspoon baking powder

½ teaspoon fine sea salt

½ cup (118 ml) canola oil

½ cup (118 ml) heavy whipping cream

½ cup (113 g) applesauce

¼ cup (57 g) sour cream

2 teaspoons lemon flavor

Zest of 1 lemon

FROSTING

3 cups (425 g) powdered sugar, sifted

½ cup (113 g) salted butter, softened

½ cup (113 g) cream cheese

1 teaspoon vanilla extract

Preheat the oven to 350°F. Line a cupcake pan with liners.

TO MAKE THE BATTER: In the bowl of a stand mixer fitted with the paddle attachment, add the cake flour, cane sugar, baking powder, and sea salt and mix on low for two to three rotations to combine the dry ingredients.

Add the canola oil, whipping cream, applesauce, sour cream, and lemon flavor and mix on low until combined into a smooth batter. Add the lemon zest and mix to combine.

Scoop the batter into the prepared pan, filling three-quarters full.

Bake for 20 to 24 minutes, until a toothpick inserted in the center comes out clean. Allow to cool completely in the pan.

TO MAKE THE FROSTING: In the bowl of a stand mixer fitted with the paddle attachment, add the powdered sugar, butter, cream cheese, and vanilla extract. Mix on low until combined and then speed up the mixer to high for 1 minute, or until light and fluffy.

Transfer the frosting to a piping bag with Ateco tip #808 or no tip. Frost the cupcakes by piping a large dollop onto each one.

Store in an airtight container in the fridge for up to 3 days.

GLUTEN-FREE

Replace the cake flour with ¾ cup (113 g) gluten-free flour blend and ¾ cup plus 2 tablespoons (85 g) coconut flour.

HIGH ALTITUDE

Bake at 350°F for 18 to 22 minutes, until a toothpick inserted in the center comes out clean.

CHOCOLATE CHIP CAKE JARS

MAKES TWELVE 9-OUNCE JARS

This simple vanilla cake complements pure vanilla bean buttercream frosting and semisweet chocolate chips. This cake may seem very simple, but trust me, it is definitely not boring. Sometimes doing the simplest thing right can be very notable. These cake jars will wow everyone, from kids to those who have a more distinguished palate.

BATTER

½ cup salted butter, softened

¾ cup (170 g) cane sugar

1 teaspoon vanilla extract

½ cup (118 ml) heavy whipping cream, room temperature

½ cup (118 ml) milk, room temperature

¼ cup (57 g) sour cream, room temperature

1½ cups (212 g) cake flour

¾ teaspoon baking powder

½ teaspoon fine sea salt

FROSTING

6⅓ cups (907 g) powdered sugar, sifted

2 cups (454 g) salted butter, softened

1½ teaspoons ground vanilla bean

2 to 3 teaspoons milk

TOPPING

1 cup (198 g) semisweet chocolate chips

Preheat the oven to 350°F. Line three 6-inch cake pans with parchment paper.

TO MAKE THE BATTER: In the bowl of a stand mixer fitted with the paddle attachment, add the butter, cane sugar, and vanilla extract. Mix on low until combined and there are no chunks of butter.

Add the whipping cream, milk, and sour cream and mix to combine.

In a separate bowl, add the cake flour, baking powder, and sea salt and whisk together. With the mixer on low, slowly add in the cake flour mixture and mix until a smooth batter forms.

Divide the batter evenly into each cake pan, about 9 ounces (255 g) each.

Bake for 20 to 24 minutes, until a toothpick inserted in the center comes out clean. Allow to cool completely in the cake pans.

TO MAKE THE FROSTING: In the bowl of a stand mixer fitted with the paddle attachment, add the powdered sugar, butter, ground vanilla bean, and milk. Mix on low until combined, then speed up the mixer to high for 1 minute, or until light and fluffy. Transfer to a piping bag with Ateco tip #864.

Remove the cakes from the pans and crumble into a medium mixing bowl. Place a small amount of cake into the bottom of each jar. Add a swirl of frosting and top with chocolate chips. Repeat this layer again for each jar; top with a lid.

Store in the fridge for up to 5 days.

GLUTEN-FREE

Replace the cake flour with 1⅓ cups (212 g) gluten-free flour blend.

HIGH ALTITUDE

Bake at 350°F for 18 to 22 minutes, until a toothpick inserted in the center comes out clean.

HONEY GRAHAM CAKE JARS

MAKES TWELVE 9-OUNCE JARS

Honey graham has been a favorite flavor of mine forever. It stems from multiple different honey cereals I used to eat as a child, as I always felt cereal was such a treat! I love using this flavor combination for a lighter dessert that's not too rich.

BATTER

½ cup salted butter, softened

¾ cup (170 g) cane sugar

1 teaspoon vanilla extract

¼ teaspoon almond extract

½ cup (118 ml) heavy whipping cream, room temperature

½ cup (118 ml) milk, room temperature

¼ cup (57 g) sour cream, room temperature

1½ cups (212 g) cake flour

¾ teaspoon baking powder

½ teaspoon sea salt

FROSTING

6⅓ cups (907 g) powdered sugar, sifted

2 cups (454 g) salted butter, softened

¼ cup (85 g) raw honey

2 to 3 teaspoons milk

TOPPING

6 honey graham crackers

Preheat the oven to 350°F. Line three 6-inch cake pans with parchment paper.

TO MAKE THE BATTER: In the bowl of a stand mixer fitted with the paddle attachment, add the butter, cane sugar, vanilla extract, and almond extract. Mix on low until combined and there are no chunks of butter.

Add the whipping cream, milk, and sour cream and mix to combine.

In a separate bowl, add the cake flour, baking powder, and sea salt and whisk together. With the mixer on low, slowly add in the cake flour mixture and mix until a smooth batter forms.

Divide the batter evenly into each cake pan, about 9 ounces (255 g) each.

Bake for 20 to 24 minutes, until a toothpick inserted in the center comes out clean. Allow to cool completely in the cake pans.

TO MAKE THE FROSTING: In the bowl of a stand mixer fitted with the paddle attachment, add the powdered sugar, butter, honey, and milk. Mix on low until combined, then speed up the mixer to high for 1 minute, or until light and fluffy. Transfer to a piping bag with no tip.

Remove the cakes from the pans and crumble into a medium mixing bowl. Place a small amount of cake into the bottom of each jar. Add a dollop of frosting and top with crushed graham crackers (use about half a graham cracker per jar). Repeat this layer again for each jar; top with a piece of graham cracker.

Store in the fridge for up to 5 days.

GLUTEN-FREE

Use gluten-free graham crackers. Replace the cake flour with 1⅓ cups (212 g) gluten-free flour blend.

HIGH ALTITUDE

Bake at 350°F for 18 to 22 minutes, or until a toothpick inserted in the center comes out clean.

CHOCOLATE MULBERRY CAKE JARS

MAKES TWELVE 9-OUNCE JARS

Growing up, we had a mulberry tree that hung over a portion of our driveway. When the branches started to make their way closer and closer to the ground, it meant they were heavy with fresh and plump mulberries. We would stand outside and eat them straight off the tree like candy. It was rare that a bowl even made it inside. On those rare occasions when the mulberries did make it inside, they would be transformed into the best topping for chocolate cake. If you can't get mulberries, blackberries will also work in these cake jars.

BATTER

½ cup (113 g) salted butter, softened

¾ cup (170 g) cane sugar

1 teaspoon vanilla extract

½ cup (118 ml) milk, room temperature

½ cup (113 g) sour cream, room temperature

¼ cup (57 g) applesauce, room temperature

¼ cup (59 ml) heavy whipping cream, room temperature

1 cup (142 g) cake flour

⅔ cup (57 g) Dutch cocoa powder, sifted

¾ teaspoon baking powder

½ teaspoon fine sea salt

FROSTING

3 cups (710 ml) heavy whipping cream

1½ cups (212 g) powdered sugar, sifted

1½ teaspoons vanilla extract

TOPPING

12 ounces (340 g) mulberries

Preheat the oven to 350°F. Line three 6-inch cake pans with parchment paper.

TO MAKE THE BATTER: In the bowl of a stand mixer fitted with the paddle attachment, add the butter, cane sugar, and vanilla extract. Mix on low until combined and there are no chunks of butter.

Add the milk, sour cream, applesauce, and whipping cream and mix to combine.

In a separate bowl, add the cake flour, cocoa, baking powder, and sea salt and whisk together. With the mixer on low, slowly add in the cake flour mixture and mix until a smooth batter forms.

Divide the batter evenly into each cake pan, about 9 ounces (255 g) each.

Bake for 20 to 24 minutes, until a toothpick inserted in the center comes out clean. Allow to cool completely in the cake pans.

TO MAKE THE FROSTING: In the bowl of a stand mixer fitted with the whisk attachment, add the whipping cream, powdered sugar, and vanilla extract. Whisk starting on low, gradually increasing speed as the mixture starts to thicken, until you are at full speed. Whisk until the frosting is light and fluffy. Transfer to a piping bag with Ateco tip #846.

Remove the cakes from the pans and break them up with your hands into a large bowl.

Fill the jars a quarter of the way with cake, then a swirl of frosting, a couple mulberries, and repeat another layer. Continue this process with the rest of the jars.

Store in the fridge for up to 3 days.

GLUTEN-FREE

Replace the cake flour with
¾ cup plus 2 tablespoons (142 g)
gluten-free flour blend.

HIGH ALTITUDE

Bake at 350°F for 18 to
22 minutes, until a toothpick
inserted in the center comes
out clean.

GLUTEN-FREE

Replace the cake flour with
1⅓ cups (212 g) gluten-free
flour blend.

HIGH ALTITUDE

Bake at 350°F for 18 to
22 minutes, until a toothpick
inserted in the center comes
out clean.

CHOCOLATE LEMON CAKE BALLS

If you like chocolate and citrus, let me introduce you to my favorite combo—chocolate and lemon! I hope you will enjoy these cake balls as much as I do.

BATTER

½ cup (113 g) salted butter, softened

¾ cup (170 g) cane sugar

1 teaspoon vanilla extract

½ cup (118 ml) heavy whipping cream, room temperature

½ cup (118 ml) milk, room temperature

¼ cup (113 g) sour cream, room temperature

1½ cups (212 g) cake flour

¾ teaspoon baking powder

½ teaspoon fine sea salt

FROSTING

Heaping 2⅓ cups (340 g) powdered sugar, sifted

¾ cup (170 g) salted butter, softened

2 teaspoons milk

2 teaspoons lemon flavor

COATING

15 ounces (425 g) milk chocolate, chopped

Preheat the oven to 350°F. Line three 6-inch cake pans with parchment paper.

TO MAKE THE BATTER: In the bowl of a stand mixer fitted with the paddle attachment, add the butter, cane sugar, and vanilla extract. Mix on low until combined and there are no chunks of butter.

Add the heavy whipping cream, milk, and sour cream and mix to combine.

In a separate bowl, add the cake flour, baking powder, and sea salt and whisk together. With the mixer on low, slowly add in the cake flour mixture and mix until a smooth batter forms.

Divide the batter evenly into the pans, about 9 ounces (255 g) each.

Bake for 20 to 24 minutes, until a toothpick inserted in the center comes out clean. Allow to cool completely in the cake pans.

TO MAKE THE FROSTING: In the bowl of a stand mixer fitted with the paddle attachment, add the powdered sugar, butter, milk, and lemon flavor. Mix on low until combined, then speed up the mixer to high for 1 minute, or until light and fluffy.

Line two baking sheets with parchment paper. Remove the cakes from the pans and add into the bowl with the frosting. Using your hands or a spatula, stir and squish in the cake until the mixture is uniform. Using your hands, form the cake mixture into about 40 balls and place on the prepared baking sheets. Place in the freezer. (I like to pop them in the freezer for 15 minutes and then go back and re-form them into smoother, more circular balls, as I have a difficult time forming them the first time! This is optional, so you can also skip this step.) Leave the cake balls in the freezer while you make the coating.

TO MAKE THE COATING: In a double boiler, add all the chocolate. Heat the chocolate until completely melted, then remove from heat.

Remove the cake balls from the freezer. Coat each ball in the chocolate and place back on the baking sheets. Repeat for all the balls. Place back in the freezer for 5 to 10 minutes. Remove and use the excess chocolate to drizzle on top. Place the trays back in the freezer for 1 hour.

Store in the fridge for up to 7 days.

GLUTEN-FREE

Replace the cake flour with 1⅓ cups (212 g) gluten-free flour blend.

HIGH ALTITUDE

Bake at 350°F for 18 to 22 minutes, until a toothpick inserted in center comes out clean.

FUNFETTI CAKE BALLS

MAKES 40 CAKE BALLS

While funfetti cake was created for children, I think it has become just as popular among adults. These adorable little cake balls are a pretty sophisticated way to eat funfetti, if I do say so myself. They are perfect for any celebration, as their bite-sized shape makes them the most irresistible kind of party treat.

BATTER

½ cup (113 g) salted butter, softened

¾ cup (170 g) cane sugar

2 teaspoons vanilla extract

½ cup (118 ml) heavy whipping cream, room temperature

½ cup (118 ml) milk, room temperature

¼ cup (57 g) sour cream, room temperature

1½ cups (212 g) cake flour

¾ teaspoon baking powder

½ teaspoon fine sea salt

FROSTING

Heaping 2⅓ cups (340 g) powdered sugar, sifted

¾ cup (170 g) salted butter, softened

⅓ cup (57 g) rainbow sprinkles

2 to 3 teaspoons milk

COATING

16 ounces (454 g) white chocolate, chopped

Rainbow sprinkles for topping

Preheat the oven to 350°F. Line three 6-inch cake pans with parchment paper.

TO MAKE THE BATTER: In the bowl of a stand mixer fitted with the paddle attachment, add the butter, cane sugar, and vanilla extract. Mix on low until combined and there are no chunks of butter.

Add the whipping cream, milk, and sour cream and mix to combine.

In a separate bowl, add the cake flour, baking powder, and sea salt and whisk together. With the mixer on low, slowly add in the cake flour mixture and mix until a smooth batter forms.

Divide the batter evenly into each cake pan, about 9 ounces (255 g) each.

Bake for 20 to 24 minutes, until a toothpick inserted in the center comes out clean. Allow to cool completely in the cake pans.

TO MAKE THE FROSTING: In the bowl of a stand mixer fitted with the paddle attachment, add the powdered sugar, butter, rainbow sprinkles, and milk. Mix on low until combined, then speed up the mixer to high for 1 minute, or until light and fluffy.

Line two baking sheets with parchment paper. Remove the cakes from the pans and add into the bowl with the frosting. Using your hands or a spatula, stir and squish in the cake until the mixture is uniform. Using your hands, form the cake mixture into about 40 balls and place on the prepared baking sheets. Place in the freezer. (I like to pop them in the freezer for 15 minutes and then go back and re-form them into smoother balls, as I have a difficult time forming them the first time! This is optional, so you can also skip this step.) Leave the cake balls in the freezer while you make the coating.

TO MAKE THE COATING: In a double boiler, add all the chocolate. Heat the chocolate until completely melted, then remove from heat.

Remove the cake balls from the freezer. Coat each ball in the chocolate and place back on the baking sheets; top with rainbow sprinkles. Repeat for all the balls. Place the trays back in the freezer for 1 hour.

Store in the fridge for up to 7 days.

CINNAMON HONEY CAKE BALLS

MAKES 40 CAKE BALLS

Cinnamon and honey has always been a combination I gravitate toward. Being a chocolate lover, I of course love to add in some chocolate. The smooth milk chocolate in this recipe complements the sweet honey and cinnamon just perfectly. This is one of those recipes I make again and again.

BATTER

½ cup (118 ml) milk

1 tablespoon (21 g) raw honey

½ cup (113 g) salted butter, softened

¾ cup (170 g) cane sugar

1 teaspoon vanilla extract

½ cup (118 ml) heavy whipping cream, room temperature

¼ cup (57 g) sour cream, room temperature

1½ cups (212 g) cake flour

¾ teaspoon baking powder

½ teaspoon fine sea salt

FROSTING

Heaping 2⅓ cups (340 g) powdered sugar, sifted

¾ cup (170 g) salted butter, softened

2 teaspoons milk

1 teaspoon cinnamon

COATING

15 ounces (425 g) milk chocolate, chopped

GLUTEN-FREE

Replace the cake flour with 1⅓ cups (212 g) gluten-free flour blend.

Preheat the oven to 350°F. Line three 6-inch cake pans with parchment paper.

TO MAKE THE BATTER: In a small saucepan, add the milk and honey. Heat on medium until the honey has dissolved; remove from heat.

In the bowl of a stand mixer fitted with the paddle attachment, add the butter, cane sugar, and vanilla extract and mix on low until combined and there are no chunks of butter. Add the honey milk, whipping cream, and sour cream and mix on low until combined, scraping the sides of the bowl as needed.

In a separate bowl, add the cake flour, baking powder, and sea salt and whisk together. With the mixer on low, slowly add the flour to the butter mixture. Continue to mix on low until incorporated, scraping down the sides of the bowl as needed. Divide the batter evenly into each cake pan, about 9 ounces (255 g) each.

Bake for 20 to 24 minutes, until a toothpick inserted in the center comes out clean. Allow to cool completely in the cake pans.

TO MAKE THE FROSTING: In the bowl of a stand mixer fitted with the paddle attachment, add the powdered sugar, butter, milk, and cinnamon. Mix on low to combine completely, then speed up the mixer to high and mix for 1 minute, or until light and fluffy.

Line two baking sheets with parchment paper. Remove the cakes from the pans and add into the bowl with the frosting. Using your hands or a spatula, stir and squish in the cake until the mixture is uniform. Using your hands, form the cake mixture into about 40 balls and place on the prepared baking sheets. Place in the freezer. (I like to pop them in the freezer for 15 minutes and then go back and re-form them into smoother balls, as I have a difficult time forming them the first time! This is optional, so you can also skip this step.) Leave the cake balls in the freezer while you make the coating.

TO MAKE THE COATING: In a double boiler, add all the chocolate. Heat the chocolate until completely melted, then remove from heat.

Bake at 350°F for 18 to
22 minutes, until a toothpick
inserted in the center comes
out clean.

Remove the cake balls from the freezer. Coat each ball in the chocolate and place back on the baking sheets. Repeat for all the balls. Place back in the freezer for 5 to 10 minutes. Remove and use the excess chocolate to drizzle on top. Place the trays back in the freezer for 1 hour.

Store in the fridge for up to 7 days.

CHOCOLATE SPRINKLE CAKE

MAKES A TWO-LAYER 6-INCH CAKE

Sometimes you just want chocolate and sprinkles. This classic birthday cake is for the chocolate lovers: simple chocolate cake, buttercream, and sprinkles—there's not much to it, but it's exactly what everyone wants. This cake is elevated with its classy two layers, as opposed to three. Having only two layers, allows for a very generous amount of frosting for that middle layer. I think that cakes with a thick frosting layer look extra fancy!

BATTER

½ cup (113 g) salted butter, softened

¾ cup (170 g) cane sugar

1 teaspoon vanilla extract

½ cup (118 ml) milk, room temperature

½ cup (113 g) sour cream, room temperature

¼ cup (57 g) applesauce, room temperature

¼ cup (59 ml) heavy whipping cream, room temperature

1 cup (142 g) cake flour

⅔ cup (57 g) Dutch cocoa powder, sifted

¾ teaspoon baking powder

½ teaspoon fine sea salt

FROSTING

3 cups (425 g) powdered sugar, sifted

⅓ cup (28 g) Dutch cocoa powder, sifted

1 cup (226 g) salted butter, softened

2 to 3 teaspoons milk

TOPPING

Rainbow sprinkles

Preheat the oven to 350°F. Line two 6-inch cake pans with parchment paper.

TO MAKE THE BATTER: In the bowl of a stand mixer fitted with the paddle attachment, add the butter, cane sugar, and vanilla extract. Mix on low until combined and there are no chunks of butter.

Add the milk, sour cream, applesauce, and whipping cream and mix to combine.

In a separate bowl, add the cake flour, cocoa, baking powder, and sea salt and whisk together. With the mixer on low, slowly add in the cake flour mixture and mix until a smooth batter forms.

Divide the batter evenly into each cake pan, about 14 ounces (397 g) each.

Bake for 30 to 34 minutes, until a toothpick inserted in the center comes out clean. Allow to cool completely in the cake pans.

TO MAKE THE FROSTING: In the bowl of a stand mixer fitted with the paddle attachment, add the powdered sugar, cocoa, butter, and milk. Mix on low until combined, then speed up the mixer to high for 1 minute, or until light and fluffy.

Place the first cake layer on a cake stand or spinner. Add a very generous amount of frosting and spread evenly. Top with the second cake layer.

Crumb coat the cake by spreading a thin layer of frosting around the entire cake to seal in the crumbs. Place the cake in the freezer for 10 minutes to harden. Remove and frost the cake with the remaining frosting.

Add rainbow sprinkles to the sides and top, or get creative!

Store in an airtight container for up to 3 days.

GLUTEN-FREE

Replace the cake flour with ¾ cup plus 2 tablespoons (142 g) gluten-free flour blend.

HIGH ALTITUDE

Bake at 350°F for 25 to 28 minutes, until a toothpick inserted in the center comes out clean.

ITALIAN CREAM CAKE

MAKES A THREE-LAYER 6-INCH CAKE

My dad always talks about an Italian cream cake my mom made while I was growing up. Yet I never once had it. I truly believe that she baked it only for the lavish black-tie parties she hosted for her friends. Therefore, I always thought this was an adult cake. Make this for your next dinner party and wow everyone when you tell them that this showstopper is made without eggs!

BATTER

½ cup (113 g) salted butter, softened

¾ cup (170 g) cane sugar

1 teaspoon vanilla extract

¼ teaspoon almond extract

½ cup (118 ml) heavy whipping cream, room temperature

½ cup (118 ml) milk, room temperature

¼ cup (57 g) sour cream, room temperature

1½ cups (212 g) cake flour

¾ teaspoon baking powder

½ teaspoon fine sea salt

TOPPING

1 cup (85 g) fine shredded unsweetened coconut

¾ cup (96 g) pecans, finely chopped

FROSTING

Heaping 2⅓ cups (340 g) powdered sugar

½ cup (113 g) salted butter, softened

½ cup (113 g) cream cheese

1 teaspoon vanilla extract

Preheat the oven to 350°F. Line three 6-inch cake pans with parchment paper.

TO MAKE THE BATTER: In the bowl of a stand mixer fitted with the paddle attachment, add the butter, cane sugar, vanilla extract, and almond extract. Mix on low until combined and there are no chunks of butter.

Add the whipping cream, milk, and sour cream and mix to combine.

In a separate bowl, add the cake flour, baking powder, and sea salt and whisk together. With the mixer on low, slowly add in the cake flour mixture and mix until a smooth batter forms.

Divide the batter evenly into each cake pan, about 9 ounces (255 g) each.

Bake for 20 to 24 minutes, until a toothpick inserted in the center comes out clean. Allow to cool completely in the cake pans.

TO MAKE THE TOPPING: Line a baking sheet with parchment paper and spread out the coconut. Bake for 3 to 5 minutes, until lightly toasted. Transfer to a bowl with the pecans and mix together. Set aside.

TO MAKE THE FROSTING: In the bowl of a stand mixer fitted with the paddle attachment, add the powdered sugar, butter, cream cheese, and vanilla extract. Mix on low until combined, then speed up the mixer to high for 1 minute, or until light and fluffy.

Place the first cake layer on a cake stand or spinner. Add a generous amount of frosting and spread evenly; top with a sprinkle of the topping mixture. Top with the second cake layer and repeat this process, then top with the third cake layer.

Crumb coat the cake by spreading a thin layer of frosting around the entire cake to seal in the crumbs. Place the cake in the freezer for 10 minutes to harden. Remove and frost the cake with the remaining frosting. Add the remaining topping to the sides of the cake.

Store in an airtight container for up to 3 days.

⊘ GLUTEN-FREE

Replace the cake flour with
1⅓ cups (212 g) gluten-free
flour blend.

▲▲ HIGH ALTITUDE

Bake at 350°F for 18 to
22 minutes, until a toothpick
inserted in the center comes
out clean.

CHOCOLATE ALMOND CAKE

MAKES A THREE-LAYER 6-INCH CAKE

Chocolate and almond are a classic flavor combination that is also very sophisticated. This simple chocolate cake is covered with a light and fluffy almond buttercream frosting and topped with chopped almonds for a nice crunch. It's a palate-pleaser that will satisfy any cake craving!

BATTER

½ cup (113 g) salted butter, softened

¾ cup (170 g) cane sugar

1 teaspoon vanilla extract

½ cup (118 ml) milk, room temperature

½ cup (113 g) sour cream, room temperature

¼ cup (57 g) applesauce, room temperature

¼ cup (59 ml) heavy whipping cream, room temperature

1 cup (142 g) cake flour

⅔ cup (57 g) Dutch cocoa powder, sifted

¾ teaspoon baking powder

½ teaspoon fine sea salt

FROSTING

3 cups plus 3 tablespoons (454 g) powdered sugar, sifted

1 cup (226 g) salted butter, softened

2 teaspoons milk

1 teaspoon almond extract

TOPPING

½ cup (71 g) whole almonds with their skins, chopped

2 ounces (57 g) dark chocolate, melted

Preheat the oven to 350°F. Line three 6-inch cake pans with parchment paper.

TO MAKE THE BATTER: In the bowl of a stand mixer fitted with the paddle attachment, add the butter, cane sugar, and vanilla extract. Mix on low until combined and there are no chunks of butter.

Add the milk, sour cream, applesauce, and whipping cream and mix to combine.

In a separate bowl, add the cake flour, cocoa, baking powder, and sea salt and whisk together. With the mixer on low, slowly add in the cake flour mixture and mix until a smooth batter forms.

Divide the batter evenly into each cake pan, about 9 ounces (255 g) each.

Bake for 20 to 24 minutes, until a toothpick inserted in the center comes out clean. Allow to cool completely in the cake pans.

TO MAKE THE FROSTING: In the bowl of a stand mixer fitted with the paddle attachment, add the powdered sugar, butter, milk, and almond extract. Mix on low until combined, then speed up the mixer to high for 1 minute, or until light and fluffy.

Place the first cake layer on a cake stand or spinner. Add a generous amount of frosting and spread evenly. Top with the second cake layer and repeat this process, then top with the third cake layer.

Crumb coat the cake by spreading a thin layer of frosting around the entire cake to seal in the crumbs. Place the cake in the freezer for 10 minutes to harden. Remove and frost the cake with the remaining frosting.

Add the chopped almonds to the sides of the cake and on the top. Drizzle with melted chocolate.

Store in an airtight container for up to 3 days.

GLUTEN-FREE

Replace the cake flour with
¾ cup plus 2 tablespoons (142 g)
gluten-free flour blend.

HIGH ALTITUDE

Bake at 350°F for 18 to
22 minutes, until a toothpick
inserted in the center comes
out clean.

PINK LEMONADE CAKE

MAKES A THREE-LAYER 6-INCH CAKE

When I was little, one of my favorite things to do was set up a lemonade stand and sling pink lemonade to people walking through the neighborhood. Yes, my entrepreneurship started at a very young age! But I never knew if the "pink" in "pink lemonade" came from strawberry or raspberry . . . and I still don't know that answer. This cake uses fresh strawberries, but you can easily make it with raspberries instead. I use a fine mesh strainer to juice a few strawberries, as just a small amount of strawberry juice added to the frosting will give it that signature pale pink hue.

BATTER

½ cup (113 g) salted butter, softened

¾ cup (170 g) cane sugar

2 teaspoons lemon flavor

½ cup (118 ml) heavy whipping cream, room temperature

½ cup (118 ml) milk, room temperature

¼ cup (57 g) sour cream, room temperature

1½ cups (212 g) cake flour

¾ teaspoon baking powder

½ teaspoon fine sea salt

Zest of 1 lemon

FROSTING

3 cups plus 3 tablespoons (454 g) powdered sugar, sifted

1 cup (226 g) salted butter, softened

2 to 3 teaspoons strawberry juice or water

TOPPING

5 ounces (142 g) strawberries

Preheat the oven to 350°F. Line three 6-inch cake pans with parchment paper.

TO MAKE THE BATTER: In the bowl of a stand mixer fitted with the paddle attachment, add the butter, cane sugar, and lemon flavor. Mix on low until combined and there are no chunks of butter.

Add the whipping cream, milk, and sour cream and mix to combine.

In a separate bowl, add the cake flour, baking powder, sea salt, and lemon zest and whisk together. With the mixer on low, slowly add in the cake flour mixture and mix until a smooth batter forms.

Divide the batter evenly into each cake pan, about 9 ounces (255 g) each.

Bake for 20 to 24 minutes, until a toothpick inserted in the center comes out clean. Allow to cool completely in the cake pans.

TO MAKE THE FROSTING: In the bowl of a stand mixer fitted with the paddle attachment, add the powdered sugar, butter, and strawberry juice. Mix on low until combined, then speed up the mixer to high for 1 minute, or until light and fluffy.

Place the first cake layer on a cake stand or spinner. Add a generous amount of frosting and spread evenly. Top with the second cake layer and repeat this process, then top with the third cake layer.

Crumb coat the cake by spreading a thin layer of frosting around the entire cake to seal in the crumbs. Place the cake in the freezer for 10 minutes to harden. Remove and frost the cake with the remaining frosting.

Slice the strawberries and top the cake with them.

Store in an airtight container in the fridge for up to 3 days.

⊘

GLUTEN-FREE

Replace the cake flour with
1⅓ cups (212 g) gluten-free
flour blend.

▲▲

HIGH ALTITUDE

Bake at 350°F for 18 to
22 minutes, until a toothpick
inserted in the center comes
out clean.

MORE EGGLESS DESSERTS

If you've baked your way through this book and you want more, make sure to check out my blog for additional eggless recipes. New recipes are added weekly: *Mimi Bakes Photos* (mimibakes photos.com). You can search by category for Eggless Recipes.

It wasn't possible for me to put every single one of my eggless dessert recipes in this book, and I wanted to focus on a lot of desserts that usually contain eggs. So, if you're eager to keep baking, I would also recommend trying this list of desserts that *usually* do not have eggs. It's a good starting point for eggless sweets that may not be labeled as eggless.

APPLE CRISP: Apple crisp is usually made of apples, butter, sugar, and sometimes oats or flour. It's a very simple dessert. To switch it up, you can always swap out the apples for any other fruit you like.

CARAMEL CANDY: Homemade caramels should be made up of only three ingredients, in my opinion: sugar, butter, and heavy whipping cream. Eggs are never involved. Make sure to stay away from recipes that call for corn syrup or water, as they are not true caramel recipes.

CHOCOLATE CLUSTERS: Any type of chocolate clusters are usually just chocolate, dried fruit, and nuts—no eggs! This type of homemade candy is easy to make and oh-so delicious!

COOKIE DOUGH: Usually most desserts with cookie dough in the name don't have eggs, as eating raw eggs is frowned upon. So when you make edible cookie dough, eggs are not involved. These desserts include cookie dough truffles, edible cookie dough, and cookie dough bars.

FROZEN YOGURT: Unlike ice cream, frozen yogurt doesn't have eggs. Homemade froyo recipes are always really fun things to make!

FRUIT PIES: With fruit pies, the usual egg culprit is just the egg wash that is used as a glaze on top of the pie crust before baking. So, if you use my Pie Wash (page 163) instead, you can probably bake grandma's apple pie recipe without using any eggs!

FUDGE: Fudge doesn't have eggs, although some recipes call for the use of marshmallows, and sometimes marshmallows can have eggs. So watch out for that.

ICEBOX CAKES: Icebox cakes are usually made of whipped cream and store-bought cookies or graham crackers. As long as you're choosing cookies without eggs, then you're good to go. These recipes are easily adaptable, so you can use whatever type of cookies you want. You can even make your own cookies from one of the recipes in this book!

NO-BAKE CHEESECAKES: Unlike traditional cheesecakes, no-bake cheesecakes don't contain eggs. Instead, they usually contain cream cheese and heavy whipping cream. As a result, most of these recipes will be eggless.

PUDDING: Pudding is usually made using cornstarch. So, unlike custard, pudding is usually free of eggs. But not always. Make sure to check the ingredients or search for recipes that say "easy pudding," as those are usually less complicated and contain fewer ingredients, so you'll have more luck there.

SHORTBREAD COOKIES: Because shortbread cookies don't have leavening, eggs are not typically used as an ingredient in them. However, some shortbreads do use eggs, so make sure to read the ingredient list.

TRUFFLES: Many truffles feature chocolate ganache or even cookie dough in the centers—meaning no eggs are used. These are a great eggless treat and super fun to make!

ACKNOWLEDGMENTS

First, I want to thank the readers of my blog and everyone who has ever enjoyed my desserts. Without you guys, I wouldn't have even known there was a need for a truly eggless baking book. And because of your requests for eggless recipes, I have also created some of my new favorite recipes! Chocolate chip cookies, sweet rolls, coffee cakes, and more will always be made eggless in my house now. So, thank you!

Thank you to Clare Pelino for yet another book together! I am so grateful for your constant support, good advice, and partnership. There's only more to come, and I'm very thankful to be working with you. I can't wait to see what's next!

Thank you to Isabel McCarthy and Countryman Press, for seeing the potential in this book and for bringing it to life. And thank you, Isabel, for recipe testing with me! And a big thanks to everyone at W. W. Norton working behind the scenes, for getting this book in the hands of people who want eggless recipes.

I also have to thank my husband, Delaney, as he is my top recipe tester and consultant. I knew that I had a winner when I baked something and he had to ask me if there were eggs in it. He is my toughest critic! But I am so thankful for that, and for him, as he's always pushing me to be better. And he's always there to help me hold a prop, snap a photo, or eat *literally* anything!

Thank you to Nancy, Shannon, Bryn, and Kristin for helping me test recipes at sea level—all of your enthusiasm for my desserts means so much to me. The fact that you are so eager to bake my recipes is the cherry on top. Sharing my love of baking is only better when I have friends that share it too.

Last, I want to thank my friends at Organic Valley—Clovis, Wendy, Jaqueline, Marina, and Tracy. Working with all of you for the last couple years has not only inspired me as a baker, recipe developer, photographer, and writer, but it has pushed me to become better at all four. Sharing my love of organic food is why I got into the food business—to show people we can eat better, we can cook better, and we can bake better. I love that there are large companies out there that feel this way too.

INDEX

239